"Tony Jeary's book could have been titled: *The Ultimate Presenter's Handbook*. It is loaded with practical advice, technical suggestions, and tools a professional presenter can begin to use immediately. A live seminar presenting this information would be worth several hundred dollars."

— ZIG ZIGLAR
The Zig Ziglar Corporation

"Every client who calls our International Speakers bureau asks for a speaker who can INSPIRE their audience. If you speak to a handful of people or a worldful, this is the most essential book you can read. We will carry it in our international catalog. Bravo, Tony Jeary!"

— DOTTIE WALTERS, President
Walters International Speakers Bureau

"Everybody knows that to reach the top these days, you have to acquire the ability to speak in public. *Inspire Any Audience* will help one learn the skill."

— TERRANCE J. McCANN, Executive Director
Toastmasters

"It is a pleasure to acknowledge Tony Jeary and his fantastic work as a first-rate business consultant and personal trainer. . . . He is a man with a deep well of skills and a treasure trove of abilities found only in those few who have persevered to achieve great success."

— DR. ROBERT H. SCHULLER
Hour of Power

Praise for the Author

"As an Adult Sunday School teacher and a businessman, I am in front of large groups regularly. Tony is a gifted coach who has helped me gain more confidence in my God-given abilities to become a more effective speaker."

—Paul Boitmann
Black and Decker

"In the training business the real skill is to inspire your audience to ACT! I've worked with Tony on several major programs. His audiences always leave inspired with a clear sense of mission."

—Henry Hirsch, Senior Project Manager
Prism Performance Systems

"Tony's exceptional ability to organize for superior results can help you with laser accuracy when it comes to hitting the target of your presentation. The tools he presents are timely, tested, and truly valuable, if you wish to take your performance to the next level."

—Richard L. Davis
Trainer/Speaker/Facilitator

"Virtually no one can escape having to speak publicly at one time or another. Tony has ideas which can help even the most fearing of speakers."

—Hilary Pluemer, Director of Field Training
H. D. Vest Investment Securities

"Tony is an unselfish teacher and presenter. He knows how to put his audience in the spotlight and enjoys coaching others to success!"

—Fred Collins, Trainer
The Heron Group

"Tony is one of the most inspiring, enthusiastic, and motivational speakers in the business today. This book gives you specific ways to pursue that standard."

—Bob Gerold, National Trainer

"Having met the 'Best of the Best' in the Speaking Industry over the last 20 years, few people are as much a 'Product of the Product' and 'Walk their Talk' as Tony Jeary. He is one of the few people who has 'been there, done that' and achieved phenomenal success in everything he has done. If you want RESULTS, listen to Tony."

—Mark Pantak
Speaker, Author, Business Coach

"Tony Jeary is a Professional's Professional. I purchased the book for each of the bank's lending officers, including myself."

—George Bradford, President/CEO
Mid-Cities National Bank

Praise for the Book

"In today's business environment, it's harder than ever to engage audiences. Tony Jeary has created a systematic, fool-proof approach that captures audiences and creates 100 percent buy-in."

—Juanell Teague
Business Coach to the Speaking Industry

"Tony Jeary has mastered the art of inspiring an audience. Anyone who wants to improve their platform skills with real, proven ideas and techniques needs this book. I recommend it without hesitation."

—Patrick O'Dooley, CSP
Former Board Member, National Speakers Association

"After six years of professional speaking, I thought I'd read and heard it all—but then Tony's secrets opened up brand new avenues for *connecting* with my audiences—what a *fantastic* tool for the professional!"

—Jane Riley
Past President of the Georgia's Speaker Association

"Jam-packed with immediately usable information which should save the reader hours of time as well as hours of frustration."

—John Bacon
Detroit News

"If this book gives you 10% of the confidence and enthusiasm in front of any group that Tony Jeary exhibits in front of all groups, it will be your best investment ever."

—Joe Hannan, Jr.
Chrysler Corporation

"Wow! This book makes it easy! Wish I'd had it years ago!"

—David Freeborn
Ketterman-Freeborn Associates

"With the exponential growth in information sources, all of which are competing for our attention, it is refreshing to read a truly helpful book that stands out. Tony's book *Inspire Any Audience* contains practical, time-tested methods and techniques illustrated by real-life experiences of Tony and the other professionals that have made a very successful career of motivating people. A definite 'must-read' if you want to 'Inspire Any Audience'."

—Jim Blood, President
Information Marketing Systems

"Jam-packed with tidbits for trainers, presenters, and meeting leaders alike."

—Jay Houghton, Senior Consultant
Automotive Marketing Consultants, Inc.

Other titles by the Author

Communication Power! in an Hour

Gaining 100 Extra Minutes a Day

Design Your Own Life

The Science of Achieving Personal Excellence (Audio Series)

The Winning Edge (Audio Series)

A 2 Z Travel (Audio Series)

Strategies for Business Peak Performance

INSPIRE ANY AUDIENCE

PROVEN SECRETS OF THE PROS FOR POWERFUL PRESENTATIONS

TONY JEARY

TROPHY
PUBLISHING

PUBLISHED BY TROPHY PUBLISHING

DALLAS, TEXAS

(214) 484-9627

LIBRARY OF CONGRESS CATALOGING-IN-PUBLICATION DATA

Jeary, Tony, 1961–

    Inspire any audience : proven secrets of the pros for powerful presentations / Tony Jeary.

       p.   cm.

    ISBN 1-883454-07-7

    1. Business presentations.   2. Public speaking.   I. Title.

HF5718.22.J43   1996

808.5'1—dc20   96–20207

                                                            CIP

Printed in the United States of America

96 97 98 99 00 LBM 9 8 7 6 5 4 3 2 1

I dedicate this work to my wife Tammy, daughter Brooke, and family for having the patience to support my dream . . . and to the many individuals who will read this work and hopefully gain insight from my years of study.

About the Author

 Since 1986, Tony Jeary has been a force in the commercial training and public speaking arenas. He has helped educate thousands of people at hundreds of companies, resulting in increased performance, growth, and prosperity for both the individuals he has touched and their respective businesses. Jeary's strength and secret to success is his ability to listen and unerringly determine his clients' needs, from which he clarifies objectives and attains goals.

Adept and comfortable as either contributor or lead designer, Jeary specializes in leading Train-the-Trainer sessions and has lead more than most in his field. He makes presenters effective! He has served as director of training for two multimillion-dollar companies and has personally designed hundreds of workshops both large and small. As a core trainer, Jeary has on countless occasions cascaded multi-level training events to audiences as small as fifty and as large as several thousand. During several such events, Jeary has helped train more than 100,000 people in less than sixty days.

Jeary's extensive domestic training experience is equaled by few in his field. He has expanded that experience to include Europe, South America, Africa, and Asia and has trained people of more than thirty nationalities representing over twenty-five countries across these continents.

Jeary works with companies such as Chrysler, Ross Roy Communications, and Oppenheimer. He currently serves as president of High Performance Resources, Inc., a contract training and consulting bureau that specializes in providing the link between the right people and the right project.

At 17, unchallenged by a public-school curriculum, Jeary began college business courses. At 18, he began his search for an applicable business education, a search that became a passion and continues today.

Jeary understands business implicitly—and does so from both the black and red sides of the ledger. He has started, bought, and/or operated more than thirty separate businesses in his career. To his clients, this means resources. Jeary lays personal claim to experience, people, substantive research sources, and state-of-the-art equipment that few, if any, individuals in his field can.

He lives by the motto, "Give value. Do more than is expected."

Need a personal presentation "coach" or a great training workshop for your company? Contact High Performance Resources at 3001 LBJ Fwy., Suite 240, Dallas, TX 75234 or call 214-484-9627 or 800-982-2509.

Acknowledgments

There are many people who made this book possible—and I am greatly appreciative of everyone that has contributed to my life and this book. What is listed below is a brief overview of the people who have influenced my life and this book. (Because of the length, I have chosen to put this list in alphabetical order.)

John Bacon (writer/trainer)—Thanks for helping me make Quarterly Product Training great! Together we have created many great presentations, and I continue to learn from each and every experience.

Buz Barlow (my attorney and one of my best friends)—I thank you for being behind me and giving me encouragement year after year.

Ken Blanchard (consultant/speaker)—Thanks for your direction and great works.

Abby Blay & John Gillis (training executives)—Thanks for supporting me and hiring me over the years. I appreciate you so much.

Reg Cavender (training coordinator and partner)—Thanks for believing in me and being such a foundation to my goals.

Judy Chaffee (speaker/trainer)—You are the best—a true professional, period! Thanks for being my friend and thanks for the green shirt.

Chrysler clients—Thanks for the many projects. It continues to be a fantastic ride. I truly appreciate the business!

Dick Clipp (speaker/trainer)—Since 1982 I have appreciated your help and friendship.

Jim & Andrea Coleman (friends and contractors)—I read and read and read. You two people have helped me comprehend more of what I have read for years.

Fred Collins (trainer/consultant)—A friend who has truly helped me grow.

Ken Copeland & Scott Wiggins (clients and friends)—Thanks for hiring me year after year.

John Davis (consultant and understudy)—Thanks for being part of my life and helping get x's in the boxes (things accomplished).

Acknowledgments

Rick Davis (trainer/consultant) — We have shared the platform in front of audiences, on camera, and in front of clients. Thanks for being great wherever we are together!

David Freeborn & Myra Ketterman (training professionals) — Thanks for your friendship, for covering for me in tight spots, and for all your help on the book.

John Graffius (creative genius) — You have become a close friend, and I am thankful for your example of how to deal with tough situations and think solutions.

Kevin Grant (marketing expert) — You've been my client, partner, friend, and business associate and continue in all these areas to be outstanding.

Derek Green (freelance writer and facilitator) — I must acknowledge that without your help this book would not have happened. We worked for months and months to get this work just right. Your discipline is very admirable.

Jay Heinlein & John Ward (the publishers) — I am forever grateful for your helping me get my experience and expertise into this current format for others to use.

Alan Jones (trainer/consultant) — Thanks for your help with desk-topping over the years.

Doug Kevorkian (consultant/trainer) — Thanks for all your words of wisdom and helping me with so many successful projects.

Jeffrey Lant (marketer/author) — Your works have boosted my effectiveness in so many areas — marketing, speaking, consulting, and more. You are a bottom-line guy.

Jeff Lewis (creative director) — For years we have worked to build great works together.

John Mason (author and speaker) — I appreciate your time in helping me get the front of the book in order.

Jim Million (former business partner and training expert) — Your relationship with me during our partnership has had a tremendously positive effect on my expertise in the business of speaking.

Paul J. Myers (founder of SMI) — Thanks for all the hundreds of audio tapes you published that helped me improve.

Mark Pantak (speaker/coach) — You have coached me for over ten years and have truly been there for me year after year. I appreciate your expertise.

David Peak (first real friend in the world; we met at age 4) — Thanks for being such a good friend and an example of the very best. I owe you forever.

Mike Perkins (financial services expert) — Your son was my daughter's first date at three weeks old. You are a great friend, past client, and consulting partner.

Billye Phariss (Rae Ann's assistant) — A thank-you goes out to you for your fast typing as we built this book.

Rae Ann Posner (our office manager and my assistant) — Your trustworthiness and dedication over the years is something I cherish and am thankful for everyday.

Price Pritchett (change expert) — Your booklets are unmatched in value. I thank you for writing *you²* and *Quantum Leap Strategies*.

Jane Riley (enthusiastic speaker) — A friend who has encouraged me and given shortcuts and direction over the years — more than she even knows.

Dee Robin (training industry expert) — Thanks for being such a good friend.

Tony Robbins (motivational trainer) — This man shared many secrets I have used. He showed me what modeling is all about. Modeling can give you experiential growth and results.

Gifford Rogers — My sincere appreciate for your international work over the years.

Tim Salladay (trainer/consultant) — Keep on being an inspiration.

Robert Schuller (inspirational minister) — You have helped me understand how to live a life with a very positive attitude. Thanks so much for being a mentor.

Gerry Spence (famous attorney) — Thanks for your book *How to Argue and Win Every Time* — I recommend it almost weekly. I have gained much value about credibility from this work.

David Sweet (consultant/trainer) — You have shown me a clear example of what I want to become.

Juanell Teague (business coach to speakers) — I have studied your works and theories, and you have extracted from my mind many of the foundational pieces of this work.

Dave Terrell (trainer/consultant) — Thanks for your friendship and enthusiasm.

Acknowledgments

Brian Tracy (motivational speaker) — Your tapes, including *The Psychology of Achievement* and other works, have given me great inspiration. The piece that has most dramatically affected my life is your one-liner suggesting you ask yourself: "What is the most valuable use of my time right now?"

Herb Vest (major client and financial services pioneer) — Thanks for all your business when I was first getting started.

Tony Walker & Sherry Boecher (training professionals) — Two great friends and business associates who inspire me daily.

Dottie Walters (world-famous speaking expert) — Your gift of service and your true willingness to share is so very unique in today's world. You have been open and willing to give and give and support me with your experiences and contacts.

Dale Ware (trainer/consultant) — The nicest guy I know . . . in the whole world!

Zig Ziglar (motivational mentor speaker) — I have followed this man for almost 15 years. He has positively affected my life and showed me how to set goals, be humble, and be a mentor.

My clients — I am who I am because of my clients. Many are my best friends. The repeat business year after year is forever appreciated.

My family (parents Stan and Linda Jeary, brother Randy Jeary, wife Tammy and daughter Brooke, grandmother Bessie Smalley, and parents-in-law Tom and Pat Norris) — Thanks for allowing me to excel in my career. You all have supported me through the years. Thanks so very, very much!

Contents at a Glance

Credits

Editor
Nancy Norris

Interior Design/Page Layout
Toni Richard, Desktop Miracles, Inc.

Cover Design
Barry Kerrigan, Desktop Miracles, Inc.

Cover Photo
Terry Ferange Photography

Cartoonist
Patrick David, The Lords of Design

Proofreading and Indexing
Desktop Miracles, Inc.

Editorial Assistants
Dave Freeborn
Myra Ketterman
Judy Chaffee
Rick Davis
Doug Kevorkian
Reg Cavender

Table of Contents

Table of Contents

PART 2 BEGINNING YOUR PRESENTATION

Table of Contents

Table of Contents

Table of Contents

Foreword

EXPECT VALUE FROM THIS BOOK!

Whether you like it or not, you most likely have to speak to people in situations a bit more intimidating than talking to your best friend on the phone or at the golf course. So, at sometime or another you will be in a position to present—an idea, a product, or an opportunity. If you have the desire, regardless of your skill level, you can read this book and take a Giant Step toward conquering your fears and becoming inspirational in front of any audience. Or simply put, you can be confident and effective in front of a group of five or five thousand.

I have invested *years* and traveled hundreds of thousands of miles gathering proven public-speaking secrets. In fact, I've trained people to present on three continents, and in more than thirty different nationalities. I have helped develop over $50,000,000 worth of training presentations. With this book, I hope to share the simple secrets I have learned over the years, including a simple process with easy-to-follow steps. Applied faithfully, these secrets will give you the ability to inspire any audience. I challenge you to study these secrets, no matter what kind of presentations you give. Remember, the best investment you'll ever make is the investment you make in yourself.

A. D. "Tony" Jeary

P.S. Even if you make your living professionally presenting, I believe that you will find dozens of helpful ideas to increase your skill level.

Introduction

This book is about succeeding at the front of the room—any room! If you're like me, you don't want your audience to hear your words; you want them to hear your words and then *act*. The fact that you're reading this now indicates that you have a desire to raise your level of expertise as a presenter. First, let me assure you that your goal is attainable and secondly, let me congratulate you for choosing this book to take you there. By reading and applying the information and techniques I have outlined, I guarantee you will become as comfortable in front of any room as you are right now reading this.

Why Inspire?

When I first began presenting I knew I lacked *something* that the other truly outstanding speakers had. Even as my skills grew, and my audiences became more appreciative and responsive, I still sensed I was missing something.

That something, I would come to find out, was *inspiration*. Every great speaker has the power to inspire. When some people speak, you can feel the power of persuasion flow through the room. The audience stirs. They *buy-in* to what the speaker has to say—they trust the speaker. But it doesn't end there. Truly great speakers do more than inspire their audience in the "feel good" sense of the word. Exceptional speakers manage to inspire their audiences to *take action*. Their audiences leave with the intention of doing something—whether it is to try to sell new homes, apply new techniques on the job, or reread the story of David and Goliath with greater understanding.

This power to inspire has many names: charisma, persuasion, allure, influence. But regardless of what we call it, it all comes down to one thing—the ability to *move* people.

Without inspiration, there can be no actionable results. With it, you will earn trust, buy-in and critical acclaim. It will be said that you possess that *certain something*.

Let me make a promise to you—if you follow the "Seven Foundational Secrets®" in this book and you take an hour or so to learn the supporting secrets I have gathered for you, you will have at your disposal the power to *Inspire Any Audience*.

In your hands is a well-organized, easy-to-follow, easy-to-use tool. Simple, fun-to-read, and to-the-point, it's more than a how-to book. It's also a valuable reference guide that you can use every time you have to present. It's a lifetime resource—whether in front of the PTA board or the board of directors. It's heavy on tips, pointers, worksheets, and checklists, and light on personal stories, philosophy, and other filler. It's "Only the good parts." Your time is of great value to you. With this in mind, this book has been organized to ensure you get exactly what you need.

> **Every great presentation contains a certain something that makes it excellent, and, if you could isolate it and repeat it, that certain something would make you a GREAT presenter.**

My system is called the "Seven Foundational Secrets" of any presentation. Seven Foundational Secrets have been engineered to earn the speaker 100 percent audience buy-in. Each member of your audience buys into your message and wants to take action on what you are sharing. This is the cornerstone of inspiring any audience.

Here is a list of the Seven Foundational Secrets that are explained in detail within the book:

Foundational Secret #1. "Funneling Process"—simply put, this is a surveying process. Its intent is to uncover your audience's hidden needs and wants in order to guarantee your presentation is on target. This process will allow you to go through a few simple steps and define clearly your objectives and your message.

Foundational Secret #2. An understanding of the "Four Subconscious Tensions" that all audiences have. Understanding how to relieve these "tensions" will increase your audience's acceptance. Audience members have a tension between (1) themselves and other audience members; (2) themselves and the instructor; (3) themselves and any materials you have for them; and (4) themselves and their environment—such as how comfortable the room is.

Foundational Secret #3. Trust. Without trust there is no buy-in. I will show you how to use "Trust-Transference" to ignite 100 percent buy-in every time you are in front of people.

By knowing your audience, what they like, who and what they trust, you can speed up the rapport process and bond quickly and more easily.

Foundational Secret #4. "Business Entertainment". This is a must. If your audience isn't captivated, you can't be assured of their full attention and without their attention, you can't be effective. People like to have fun—think about why so many people (adults, too) flock to Disneyland. "Business Entertainment" can be achieved in many ways which are described within. But for now just think of it as "The Fun Factor."

Foundational Secret #5. "Verbal Surveying." This is used to get feedback during your entire presentation—whether it is a fifteen-minute speech, a three-day training seminar or a two-hour sales presentation. By simply asking your audience, you can know how the pace of the delivery is for them or if are you covering your subject in the right amount of detail. This allows you to adjust as you are moving through your presentation and helps insure you are on the mark.

Foundational Secret #6. "Targeted Polling." This is a process through which you decrease nervousness, relate to your audience, and establish advocates among participants. Many presenters miss the opportunity to talk one-on-one with the audience members. You can do this before you start, during breaks, and after your presentation. By polling or questioning a few people individually, you accomplish a great deal. People like to have individual attention. Make this opportunity work for you.

Foundational Secret #7. "Audience Closure." Proper closure proves you met and exceeded your audience's expectations. Executed properly, closure ensures that participants leave your presentation as ambassadors of both you and your subject matter.

HOW TO USE THIS BOOK

Inspire Any Audience: Proven Secrets of the Pros is designed for maximum effectiveness. The book is divided into four chronological parts: (1) presentation development, which begins before a word is uttered; (2) the presentation beginning; (3) the body of the presentation; and (4) the conclusion of your presentation.

You can:

➤ Spend a few minutes thumbing through the book to get familiar with its flow

➤ Address a specific need such as dealing with nervousness by going right to that chapter—or to a certain part before you start chapter one.

➤ Read the book through to get the entire process.

➤ Study just the Foundational Secrets.

➤ Use it as a lifelong reference book.

➤ Use the last two chapters alone and get something more informative than most books offer. Let me describe the last two chapters.

Extra Bang for Your Buck

First, chapter 13, entitled "Continuous Improvement," assembles a broad array of tools to evaluate yourself. These tools presented are on separate pages so you can maximize each by simply making copies straight from the book. Remember what I said about wanting you to get value and exceeding your expectations? I include in this chapter a list of my personal descriptions and evaluations of other products—the other how-to books, tapes, and magazines that I have used successfully. They are resources for *you* that you may not even know exist. Many search for years in the dark without knowing where to turn. With this book and the resources in chapter 13, you won't be one of them! This chapter concludes with a list of associates of mine who are professionals that you might want to contract for individual coaching, in your hometown or an area nearby.

Second, chapter 14 is special to me. It features eighteen perforated cards—on card stock. You can simply tear out those pages and instantly, you have eighteen special cards that contain, in bulleted format, the top secrets revealed throughout the text. These secrets, some simple, some not so simple, should save you hundreds of hours worth of research. They are the result of ten years spent collecting ideas to perfect my own presentations, plus many tips discovered by other professional speakers. This chapter contains the real answers to improving your skill level as a presenter. Go ahead; look back there if you haven't yet. You'll see what I mean.

A Special Note: Even More Bang for Your Buck

I designed this book to make it friendly, useful, and valuable to you. For those of you who like a little variety, the book is jam-packed with boxed notes throughout, pictures to better explain a concept, quotes, and tons of checklists. In many chapters, you will find a mini-essay or two. I called on a few of my colleagues to provide their unique perspectives. I gathered reinforcements to make sure I could exceed your expectations.

PART 1
Before Your Presentation

This chapter reveals:

➤ How to really understand what your audience members think, want, and expect

➤ Why it is critical to identify your objectives before you begin developing your presentation

➤ How to use the "Funneling Process": five simple steps that will help you define your objectives and get you ready to develop your presentation

1

Defining Your Objectives

"Would you tell me please, which way I ought to go from here?"

"That depends a good deal on where you want to get to."

— Lewis Carrol, *Alice in Wonderland*

The Scene . . .

You've just received a call from your boss. Because you've done such a good job this year, she has chosen YOU to give a presentation. The only problem is, just because you're good at your job doesn't make you a trained presenter.

Or, you volunteer to help with Sunday school activities. One of the things you have to do is lead a half-day seminar. But whenever you sit down to write out your ideas, your mind goes blank.

Or, you finally have the chance to make a few extra dollars in a way that's worked for many of your friends. However, you have to give "opportunity presentations." You get a few bits of information from

3

here and there to prepare. But you just don't feel like you have that certain way that makes presenting so easy for some of the people you know.

Or, there's a big presentation in your biology class. You know the material. You've not been ready in the past. This time you're going to do better...

The Solution ...

For all those scenes and hundreds like them is something I call the "Funneling Process." It takes all the things you might do—those

Information Goes in the Top Here and Is Funneled Down Through the Steps

1. **Determine the action** you want your audience to take.
   - Ask yourself, "What action do I want my audience to take as a result of my presentation?"
   - Ask yourself, "What must the participants know, say, and do differently when they leave my presentation?"

2. **Define your audience.**
   - You must know the audience very well.
   - Ask yourself, "What are the skills, knowledge, and attitudes of my audience?"
   - What are the positions represented in the audience?

3. **Brainstorm to determine:** • Your needs
   - Your audience's needs • Any third-party needs

4. **Focus these various desires**—work them into three or four *written* objectives, keeping in mind that participants want practical, usable knowledge.
   - Keep objectives short.
   - Write out in one sentence what you want to accomplish. Refer to it often.

5. **Test your objectives mentally** by putting yourself in the audience's shoes. Once you've defined your audience, check your objectives from their perspective.

Result = Core Objectives of Your Presentation

"With well-written, meaningful, and measurable objectives, the trainer has the course practically designed."

When you have your objectives on target you can really inspire. When I'm starting to define objectives for a presentation, I use a proven process that I think you will find very valuable, whether you are in an auditorium talking with hundreds of people or in a business meeting with just a few in attendance!

—from *7 Steps to Building Better Training* by Martin M. Broadwell

hundreds of possibilities that daze and paralyze you like a deer caught in headlights—and funnels them down to a solid core of doable, reachable objectives. Another way of looking at it: Most of us are very good at accomplishing a handful of small chores once we know what they are. The problem with coming up with a new presentation—for the novice and for the master alike—is deciding where you're going to go and how to get there.

The funneling process will solve this problem.

Get Started by Using the "Funneling Process" to Define Your Objectives!

Step 1. Determine the Action

The first important step for developing clear objectives is to determine the action you wish your audience to take. There are three basic "actions" that you can aim for when giving a presentation.

1. You want the audience to change an attitude.

2. You want the audience to learn something (knowledge).

3. You want the audience to attain or perfect a skill.

For clarification ask yourself:

➤ Will you be trying to *change an attitude* among your listeners (a keynote address, motivating some associates or friends to action, a presentation at a manager's meeting, talking to a DARE group for teenagers, addressing the local PTA about school-lunch programs)?

➤ Are you trying to *impart some knowledge* to your listeners (as in teaching Sunday School, coaching your child's baseball team, or making a presentation to your sales staff)?

➤ Is there a skill you are
trying to transfer to the
audience (perhaps in a
dance class, or a presen-
tation to a hobby group
or a rotary club, or in
training fellow workers
in your department)?

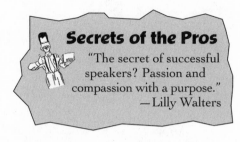

Secrets of the Pros

"The secret of successful
speakers? Passion and
compassion with a purpose."
—Lilly Walters

Once you've written down what you wish to accomplish, you're
ready to define your audience.

Step 2. Define Your Audience

To create audience buy-in for your presentation you have to give
your audience a good REASON to listen to you—and that reason
has to do with what they can GET from you. Audiences have to
have a selfish reason to listen to you or they'll simply walk away.
Remember—your audience is like you. That means their time is
valuable. Why *should* they listen unless you can give them something
at least as valuable as their time? This means that from your audience's viewpoint your presentation has to answer a simple question:
"What's in it for me?" But in order to answer the question yourself—to know what's in it for your audience—you must first know
who your audience is. That's why you must define your audience.

To get an idea of what your audience will look like, complete the
following checklist as soon as you find out you're going to be giving
a presentation.

❑ Create a profile of the average audience member—include age,
background, marital status, education, income and job.

❑ Create a list of people your audience would likely admire—this
can give you great insight.

❑ Talk with former attendees of the same types of presentations.

❑ Talk with former presenters who've addressed similar groups.

❑ Interview the client or event planner if one is available.

❑ Request a list of likely audience members—then pre-poll them
by calling in advance to see what they expect.

Follow these steps even when you think you know the audience. A clear understanding of who makes up the audience is the foundation for your entire presentation. Be thorough!

Although each audience you encounter is unique, there are seven subconscious desires that are shared by all audiences.

The Seven Subconscious Desires of Your Audience

Everyone in your audience is a human being and wants:

1. To belong

2. To be respected

3. To be liked

4. To be safe

5. To succeed

6. To find romance

7. To be inspired (enthused)

To begin Step 2: Ask yourself, "What are the skills, knowledge, and attitudes of my audience?"

Four Levels of Learning a Skill

1. **Unconscious Incompetence** — A time when the learner is not only unaware of skill, but moreover wouldn't be good at it if he were aware. A baby doesn't know about tying his shoe and couldn't tie it if he did.

2. **Conscious Incompetence** — The learner is aware of the skill, but nevertheless cannot perform it. A child becomes aware of Mom and Dad tying shoes, but he can't do it.

3. **Conscious Competence** — The learner is aware of the skill and can consciously perform it. A child can tie it's shoe, but sticks it's tongue out because it has to think about it.

4. **Unconscious Competence** — The learner performs the skill without thinking about it. It becomes an automatic response. A child ties his shoes without thinking about it.

Knowing your audience is a critical step toward knowing how to satisfy their needs. Too often, presenters skip this crucial step. Don't make this mistake! Understand your audience's needs and the actions you want them to take to meet those needs even before you begin to develop your presentation. The time you invest now will pay big dividends later.

Presentation audiences are *active*—or at least they ought to be. Audience members generally come in one of four different types. Explaining the four types and acknowledging the mental state (or tension) of participants lets them know it's OK to be in whatever mind set they're in. It also relaxes you and the audience and adds credibility to yourself as a professional, letting participants know that you realize where their heads are.

David Freeborn uses a fun technique to address the four types of participants up front. He begins by saying, "Having presented seminars all over the world to all different types of people, I've discovered that participants typically fall into four basic categories or mental states.

"First, we have *The Prisoner.* This is the person who does not particularly want to be here today. In fact, he would rather be *anywhere* than indoors listening to another talk. Someone else made that decision for him by sending him to this seminar. It's OK if you're a Prisoner. We welcome all Prisoners because that only means you are not responsible for *being* here today . . . but you *are* responsible

Recently, I was asked by one of my major clients to redesign a multimillion-dollar program for new franchisees. I took the assignment only after the client agreed I could have the time needed to survey the audience. I wanted to know everything I could about them—even though I had prepared work for this type audience before. As a result of my survey efforts, I found out some things that were pertinent to the business at hand. I was able to understand the current needs of the audience and to create accurate objectives thereby increasing the likelihood of a successful presentation.

How to identify the four types of audience members

Prisoner—Look for crossed arms, both literally and figuratively.

Vacationer—Look for a general good mood combined with an overrelaxed attitude.

Graduate—Look for frowns, rolling eyes, smug looks, and crossed arms.

Student—Look for smiles, enthusiastic nodding, and the merciful habit of laughing at your jokes.

for what you take out of here! May I see a show of hands as to how many Prisoners we have here today?

"Next, we have *The Vacationer.* This is the person who volunteers to go to any seminar, figuring it's better to be in a meeting than at work, home, or wherever else he'd normally be. In other words, he's happy to be here, but for the wrong reasons. And we're happy to have our Vacationers on board today because they like to have fun, and we'll count on them to help us have a good time. How many Vacationers do we have with us today?

"Then there's *The Graduate.* This is the person who thinks he doesn't need to be here because he already knows this stuff. But we're glad to have the Graduates, too, because this is the place for them to share all their knowledge and wisdom with others.

"Finally, we have *The Student.* This is the attentive, hardworking, perfect participant who wants to hear what you've come to say. He is eager to learn and share and, like a sponge, ready to absorb all he can to help him be more effective personally and professionally. We always welcome the students!"

Some audience members will represent a combination of these traits—but most will fit nicely into one of the categories.

Once you've done your basic audience research, fill out the form on page 11. This will give you a single audience reference page throughout the entire period you spend developing your presentation.

Step 3. Brainstorm to Determine Wants

At this point you have taken two steps.

1. You've decided what action you wish your audience to take.

2. You've begun to define what kind of audience members you'll have.

When developing your objectives, keep in mind that all presentations must meet the needs of three distinct audiences. Success or failure is determined to one degree or another by how well your objectives meet the needs of these "audiences." The three audiences are:

1. **Attendees**—those lucky folks who get to hear you.

2. **Any interested third parties**—this group can include but is not limited to clients, bosses, parents, friends, family, or anyone with a vested interest in how well your presentation turns out.

> **Secrets of the Pros**
> "When in doubt, take a survey."
> —Dottie Walters

3. **You**—the life of the party.

To use this information, try the following. Sit down at a table with three sheets of paper. At the top of one write: "The Audience." At the top of the second write: "Third Parties." And on the third sheet write: "Me." Under each heading write down the essential needs that must be satisfied for that group. By essential, I mean those things that, without which, you might as well not even give the presentation. Next write down those things that are important to have—the sorts of things that would really make the presentation shine. Then write down the things that would really make you a star; elements that anyone in any of the three audiences would consider to be above and beyond the call of duty.

Write freely—at this stage you're just brainstorming. Try to fill each page. If you fill one side of the sheet, turn it over and continue. Remember, this is raw resource material—you're simply trying to determine every possible need that your participants, any third parties, and you might have of your presentation. If you've

AUDIENCE WORKSHEET

What sort of knowledge about my topic do they bring to the table?

_____

_____

_____

Will they be for me or against me? Why?

_____

_____

_____

List of people whom they admire in their organization and are most likely to admire outside of it:

_____

_____

_____

Things that have worked with similar audiences in the past—and things that haven't:

_____

_____

_____

Why was I asked to present?

_____

_____

_____

gone off in numerous directions, written half-sentences, misspelled words, or come up with a bunch of unrelated ideas—congratulations! You're doing exactly what you ought to be doing—letting your brain storm off in any direction it chooses.

Once you've finished this step, set the paper aside and don't look at it for at least an hour or two—longer if possible. This will give you time to gain perspective on the raw material that will eventually become your focused objectives.

Step 4. Focusing Needs into Objectives

Step 3, brainstorming your audience's needs, was the creative part of developing your objectives. Step 4 is the rational part—where you take all the ideas and raw material you've generated and focus it into solid, CLEAR objectives.

First, review the material you brainstormed while trying to focus on the *most important* needs on your lists and possible ways of satisfying those needs. Identify ten to twelve different ideas, if possible. Once you've identified what's most important, you're ready to convert this raw material into objectives.

To do so, you will need to answer the following questions:

- Why am I giving this presentation?
- What's in it for my audience(s)?
- What is the purpose of the presentation?
  - ☞ To inform your audience
  - ☞ To instruct them
  - ☞ To persuade them
  - ☞ To entertain them
  - ☞ All of the above
- What do I want my audience(s) to say after the presentation?
- What do I want my audience(s) to believe?
- What *specific* action do I want my audience(s) to take?

Once you've answered these questions you're prepared to write your objectives. Do so in three short, concise sentences. These sentences—your objectives—should address the WHAT, HOW, and WHY of your presentation:

➤ WHAT will be the actual content of the presentation?

➤ HOW detailed will the information in the presentation be and HOW long will the presentation last?

➤ WHY will audience members wish to act when they leave the presentation?

Secrets of the Pros

"I like to get my talk down to three or four 'big hit' things that people can take home with them—like the way I write. I think people fall to sleep with lists. Whenever a speaker starts off with, 'Here are ten points I'm going to make . . .' I go into snoozeville."

—Dr. Ken Blanchard

Your sentences should be as short and clear as possible. Avoid weak and vague phrases like, "To become familiar with five answers to Problem X." Instead, use action words that give clear directions: "To identify the five steps

One true sentence

Many presenters like to write a mission statement as part of their objectives. A mission statement is one sentence that sums up the presentation and what it will accomplish:

"To provide an entertaining atmosphere for learning sales techniques that will increase audience members' product awareness and increase their income."

You should strongly consider trying to sum up YOUR presentation in one single sentence and then refer back to it repeatedly. It keeps your eyes on the prize and lets you remained focused on the big picture while you're working out the details.

I've always used a basic preparation format for developing presentation objectives. I imagine myself planning a trip.

1. What is the **destination** (the conclusion or action required)?
2. What **route** (amount of detail and information)?
3. What **speed** do I need to drive?
4. Why am **I driving?**
5. Why are we **going on the trip?**

I wouldn't go to Disneyland without a few clear reasons and directions. Why would I give a presentation with less?

—Fred Collins

needed to resolve Problem X." The clearer and more specific your three objectives, the easier it will be for you to develop your presentation.

Again, limit yourself to *three sentences;* anything else is too much to try to accomplish in a single presentation. It's easy to give in to the temptation to overpack a presentation. Avoid the temptation! An overpacked presentation creates an overwhelmed audience, resulting in a loss of interest during your presentation and virtually zero retention. Providing just the right amount of information begins with the creation of clear and focused objectives.

Step 5. Test Your Objectives Mentally

Once you've written down your three objectives, test them by putting yourself in your audience's shoes. Remember: each participant wants to know, "What's in it for me?" To make sure your objectives address this question, ask yourself the following questions:

Secrets of the Pros

"How many of you here are here because someone made you come? Sales manager, owner, boss, spouse, maybe someone told you 'needed' to come? (You just got 90% paying attention to you.)"

—Steve Richards

➤ Are my objectives clear?

➤ Do I know WHAT I want to accomplish, HOW I want to accomplish it, and WHY I want to accomplish it?

➤ Have I used ACTION words that describe what my presentation will do?

➤ Do my objectives give participants a good reason to listen?

Your presentation is primarily geared toward your participants. Though objectives must address your needs and the needs of any third party, the most important group is your immediate audience. Make sure your objectives work for them.

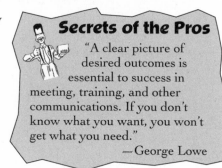

Secrets of the Pros

"A clear picture of desired outcomes is essential to success in meeting, training, and other communications. If you don't know what you want, you won't get what you need."

—George Lowe

Keep It Simple!

"The art of art, the glory of expression and the sunshine of the light of letters is simplicity."

—Walt Whitman, *Leaves of Grass*

"Keep It Simple, Stupid."

—Anonymous

Okay, so there are elegant and not-so-elegant ways of saying the same thing. But Walt Whitman and our anonymous poet both offer the same truth: The simple way is usually the best way to get a job done. There's something marvelous about solving a complex problem with a simple solution—and the same is true for any presentation.

When creating your objectives, be reasonable in your expectations of yourself and of your audience: go for the goal you can achieve in the real, not the

Secrets of the Pros

"Move them to make a decision every time you stand up."

—Tim Salladay

ideal, world. When writing those objectives down, strive for clarity and simplicity; this creates an impression of confidence and precision, while relieving the audience of work. And when addressing your audience, use the simple, plain, and powerful language of everyday talk to get your job done. Remember: we want them to want you back. Make your presentation memorable by trading in pompous complexity for saintly simplicity.

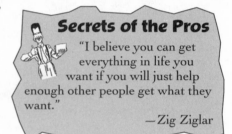

Secrets of the Pros

"I believe you can get everything in life you want if you will just help enough other people get what they want."

— Zig Ziglar

In Summary

Your objectives are the signposts, not the destination of your presentation. Would you go on a long trip without at least glancing occasionally at the road signs? Probably not. But too many presenters like to jump in and start developing the nitty-gritty details of a presentation before they've carefully considered where they're going and why. This results in an unfocused, confusing presentation that, in a "best-case scenario" gets reworked; and in a "worst-case scenario," fails.

Avoid both scenarios by creating clear objectives at the outset, then delivering on them in your presentation!

Very Important Points to Remember

✔ Clear objectives are the bedrock of a good presentation—without them, a presentation lacks focus, direction, and value.

✔ Create objectives by following the steps outlined in the funneling process.

✔ Objectives should be short, well-focused, and answer these three questions: WHAT will you present? HOW will you present it? and WHY should the audience listen?

✔ When developing your objectives, know your immediate audience. They have one basic question: "What's in it for me?"

Fill in Your Favorite Tips from the Chapter

✔ _____

_____

✔ _____

_____

✔ _____

_____

✔ _____

_____

This chapter reveals:

➤ How to build a three-dimensional outline from your objectives

➤ How to develop a complete presentation from scratch

➤ How to effectively rehearse what you developed

2

Developing and Rehearsing Your Presentation

JEARY THEORY

To build a great presentation you start by building a great outline that includes timing along with the whats, whys, and hows of the presentation—then you rehearse with it.

"It isn't the will to win that's important. Everyone has the will to win. What's important is the will to *prepare* to win."

—Bobby Knight

The Scene ...

You've decided to take the services your small independent firm offers and present them in person to prospective clients. You already know what your top three objectives are, because you used the Funneling Process outlined in chapter 1 of this book. Now you have your objectives figured out, but that doesn't mean you know how to turn those into a well-prepared, flexible, and entertaining presentation.

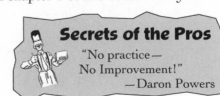

Secrets of the Pros

"No practice—
No Improvement!"
—Daron Powers

19

The Solution . . .

Is to turn your objectives into a presentation. If you haven't determined your presentation objectives, turn to chapter 1, and take some time to do so. If you're clear on your objectives, then proceed through the two-part process outlined below. Part one will take you from blank paper to full-fledged presentation. Part two will show you the best way to maximize your time by detailing effective ways to rehearse and hone your presentation.

Secrets to Developing Your Presentation

1. Start with the top three objectives you developed using the Funneling Process from chapter 1. Presentations will be built around these.

2. Define your limitations with the following questions:
   ➤ *How* much time will you have to prepare?
   ➤ *How* much time will you have to speak?
   ➤ *What* kind of room will you be speaking in?
   ➤ *What* is the financial budget: large, small or non-existent?
   ➤ *What* equipment will you have available?

3. Build a "Three-Dimensional Outline." It should have at least four columns with the following headings, running left to right:
   TIME   **WHAT**   **WHY**   **HOW**

4. Decide on, then apply, a logical sequence to your presentation. Some of the more widely used sequences are:
   ➤ Past to present
   ➤ Priority (relative importance of various topics)
   ➤ Pain to pleasure
   ➤ Categorical
   ➤ Comparison and contrast
   ➤ Advantages and disadvantages
   ➤ Ideal vs. reality

5. Pare back any point that takes more than fifteen minutes to explain. Keep your pacing fast and your ideas simple.

6. Identify and secure the best tools your budget will allow to get your point across.

7. Brainstorm and review your material with other developers (if possible).

Start with Crystal-Clear Objectives

Begin developing your presentation by reviewing the sheet that summed up your top three objectives in chapter 1. These will drive the creative process. Objectives are as varied as presentation topics themselves, but some examples of objective summations could look like this:

For a presentation on Freudian psychology:

1. Identify the three top concepts for this year's psychological convention: the ego, the id, and the super-ego.

2. Ensure audience buys-in to the three concepts and retains at least one major point about each.

3. Excite the audience about these three ideas and inspire them to learn more about them.

For a presentation on the relevance of the biblical story "David and Goliath":

➤ Create excitement among listeners for this and other Bible stories.

➤ Make sure that the listeners understand and retain the reading of David and Goliath as a lesson on perseverance and determination.

➤ Instruct listeners in the notion of "interpretation" and what it means to them. Close with them having an understanding of why stories like this matter to them.

Presentation differs from other modes of communication in the following way: you *present* your objectives by delivering **short and memorizable** pieces of information. This is one of the major ways a presentation differs from a book. Always remember that presentation audiences want:

➤ Practical, usable knowledge.

➤ Information presented in an easy-to-remember format.

A writer's job is to deliver all of the details—the rules and their exceptions, the research, the analysis, the facts, figures, and data for the reader to digest and use at some future time. The presenter's job is to think that material out and to make something that impacts a listener now. A presentation is immediately actionable and, if closed properly, includes a call to action. This action orientation is accomplished partly in the way the presentation is delivered in clearly delineated and easily digestible parts. These parts or segments include:

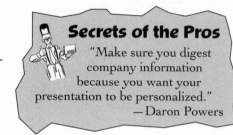

➤ Introduction
➤ Body
  • subsection one
  • subsection two
  • subsection three (and so on)
➤ Close

No rocket science here. But the trick is to make sure that each part and each subsection of your presentation does the job it's meant to do. For now, it's important to remember that a presentation is made up of SECTIONS joined together by TRANSITIONS. By dividing material into sections your mind can digest and sort it better. Think of a phone number in three sections, as area code, prefix and four numbers. (For an in-depth discussion of the various SECTIONS of your presentation, what they ought to accomplish, and how to accomplish them, see the appropriate chapter—Introduction: chapter 4; Body: chapter 10; Close: chapter 12.)

What Then?

This first concrete step in developing a presentation is to decide what you're going to say. This is where most people get stuck. This is usually because all the possible information you can present, directions you can take, and approaches you can use are so numerous. There's just too much to choose from, and that is overwhelming. The best way to ease this panic is to begin sorting through this wide range of possibilities. Do this by filling out a worksheet I like to call a "presentation work order" (see facing page).

This gives you a realistic idea of what your limitations are. And a clear idea of your limitations automatically helps you sort out what

THE PRESENTATION WORK ORDER

Title of Presentation _____

Date of Presentation _____

How much time do I have to prepare? _____

How much time will I have to speak? _____

What kind of room will I be speaking in?

❏ Conference room   ❏ Living room

❏ Boardroom   ❏ Other _____

❏ Classroom

How many people will I be speaking to? _____

What type of financial budget is available?

❏ Large budget—lots of money, as in   <u>$ Let's do it right!</u>
   "Money is no (big) object."

❏ Small budget—money is available $_____
   but is definitely an object.

❏ No budget—money isn't an object $_____0_____
   because there's none to spend.

What type of equipment will be available to me?

❏ Flip chart(s)?   ❏ Overhead projector?

❏ Tape player?   ❏ VCR and monitor?

❏ Advanced presentation   ❏ Chairs and tables?
   hardware and software?

❏ Other _____

What type of equipment do I need to provide / rent? _____

_____

What about handouts? _____

_____

This page may be reproduced without permission.

you can and can't say. Once you know how much time you have to prepare and how much time you'll have to deliver your presentation, you will see the general shape that your presentation will eventually take. Bring it further into focus by creating a . . .

Three-Dimensional Outline

The three-dimensional outline is special. The difference between a standard outline and a three-dimensional outline, is that the latter indicates not only what you want to say, but also when, why, and how to say it; making it an indispensable part of any presentation preparation.

This three-dimensional outline or matrix, lets you see the "big picture" and allows you to begin sorting through the material you'll have to produce right away. On the following pages, I provide you with a simple blank sheet for filling in your "first draft"

> **Secrets of the Pros**
>
> "There are always three speeches, for every one you actually gave: The one you practiced . . . the one you gave . . . the one you wish you gave!"
> —Dale Carnegie

presentations. The first two pages show a sample matrix created by two imaginary presenters Sigmund and Carl who are charged with giving a team presentation. The third page shows an example of a complex matrix that is designed for a longer presentation with lots of material and more than one presenter.

These complex 3-D outlines can be tailor-made (on a computer or by hand) to fit your presentation's own specifications. Remember to start with a simple matrix (like the one that follows) so that you can get things blocked out in order to see the big picture. Remember, time is precious in your presentation. The 3-D outline allows you to make the most of that valuable commodity.

Complete each column with the following information:

➤ **TIME:** This is the amount of time you'll have to cover a segment (e.g., your introduction, your agenda, your three top points, etc.)

➤ **WHAT:** This is what you will cover in that time. At this stage, you will want to include just the main points you can cover in your allotted TIME.

➤ **WHY:** This is the reason you have chosen WHAT you will say and the TIME you will spend saying it.

➤ **HOW:** This includes the method of delivering (e.g., video, overheads, role plays)

The 3-D Outline

Title of Presentation: _____

Date of draft: _____

Objectives of Presentation:

• _____

• _____

• _____

TIME Allotted	WHAT	WHY	HOW
5 min.	Welcome	Relaxation	Talk
7 min.	Show Opening Video	Vary Media	Video
10 min.	Icebreaker	Excitement	Game
30 min.			
15 min.			
10 min.	Break		

The sample matrix above will get you started.

Developing Your Presentation

SAMPLE 3-D OUTLINE

Title of Presentation: Ego, Super-ego, and Id: Today's Mind

Objectives:

1. To identify the three top concepts for this year's psychological convention: the ego, the id, and the super-ego.

2. To ensure audience buys-in to the three concepts and retains at least one major point about each.

3. To excite the audience about these three ideas and inspire them to learn more about them.

TIME	WHO*	SEGMENT	WHAT	WHY	HOW
3 min.	CARL		Welcome	Grab attention and revel commitments	Intro
7 min.	CARL		Show opening video	Keep interest	Video
10 min.	SIGMUND	I N T R O	Icebreaker; paper-tear activity	Involve audience	Game
30 min.	SIGMUND		Introduce key concepts for the day: • EGO • ID • SUPER-EGO	Introduce important concepts to learn	Overheads
3 min.	CARL		Present day's agenda: where we're going next		
10 min.			Break	Refresh audience	

Note how this organizer has included a column for extra speakers and a column for reminding himself which segment he is currently delivering.

* Include this category when featuring more than one speaker,

Decide on Logical Sequence to Your Presentation

Take a look at everything you have in front of you.[1] By now you've determined what type of audience you have. You've completed your objectives. You've filled in the presentation work order, and gotten an idea of what will and won't be a part of your presentation. Now, you need to decide on how you're going to sequence the material.

The sequences below are the most common arrangements for organizing the material you'll present. You can use just one, or mix-and-match them to suit the specific type of material or audience you're dealing with—remember, variety is the spice of life.

Past to present: this method presents material chronologically. This method works well when you need to cover historical periods, or trace the development of a product, position, or concept.

Priority: this method presents material in order of its relative importance.

Advantages and disadvantages: presents a point in such a way to show its up side and down side. This is especially good for presenting controversial material or for when you're presenting to inform an individual or group before a decision is made.

Pain to pleasure: this method takes the audience through an unfortunate but correctable situation along with a list of possible solutions.

Categorical: this method requires the creation of categories for your material. You might organize your material into sections such as "Features and Benefits", "Competitive Comparisons", or "Heroes and Villains." The categorical arrangement is good when you have a lot of complex points that need to be presented simply.

> **Secrets of the Pros**
>
> "Know your audience. There is not a successful salesperson alive today that does not go into a potential customer's office unprepared."
> —Sherry Boecher

---

1. Starting to generate a lot of paper? Visit your local office supply to pick up a plastic-covered three-ring binder. Title it (especially the spine) with your presentation's title, date it, and begin to file the worksheets and pages you generate. This will provide you with an easy-to-access record.

Experiment with these arrangements. Again, try to use more than one for a presentation that lasts more than an hour. Different segments can be presented using different sequences. Your introduction might employ Past to Present;

Secrets of the Pros

"The paradox faced by every presenter is that it takes considerable preparation in order to be spontaneous."
—Bob Gerold

then your opening segment might launch off in a Priority sequence. And you might close with Pain to Pleasure. The key is to have fun and create variety! Your audience will appreciate it.

On the following page is a large matrix for you to record a very long (one full day or longer) presentation.

THREE-DIMENSIONAL OUTLINE

Title of Presentation: _____

Objectives:

- _____
- _____
- _____

Time	Who	Segment	What	Why	How

REHEARSING YOUR PRESENTATION

What Is Effective Rehearsal?

Having a solid outline for your presentation is absolutely necessary, but it does not complete your preparation. The single most critical step is rehearsal. A great presenter always appears to be comfortable, relaxed, and in control. It looks easy for her. This relaxed, controlled demeanor is not so much the result of natural poise as it is effective rehearsal. Many think they are rehearsing by reading over notes, studying subject material, or memorizing parts of the presentation. All of this helps, but these steps alone do not constitute effective rehearsal.

> **Effective rehearsal means making the best of your preparation time to become comfortable, relaxed, and in control—both mentally and physically. It also means anticipating and avoiding troubles before they happen.**

Without effective rehearsal you run the risk of undoing all the hard work you've put into your presentation up to this point.

Seven Simple Steps to Rehearse Your Presentation

1. Mentally walk through your presentation using the 3-D outline/matrix.

2. Use 3x5 cards of key points, times, and directions while rehearsing.

3. Audio or videotape practice sessions. Study your expressions and tone.

4. Rehearse in front of someone (associates, spouse, friend).

5. Rehearse with the equipment you'll use (pointer, flip chart, overheads).

6. Know your room: walk the room before your presentation at the actual rehearsal site.

7. Sit in the audience seating to get a feel for the room.

The Mental Walk-Through

Great athletes all know how important a mental walk-through is. After the 1972 Olympics, Mark Spitz was asked to account for his great success as a swimmer. He explained that he had imagined himself swimming every lap of every event months before the event took place. Great skiers, boxers, runners, and football players tell similar stories. If imagination works in sports, the most physical of all endeavors, it can do wonders for your performance at the front of the room.

When mentally walking through your presentation, first imagine how long you will speak, and how you might begin. Then proceed to the next segment. This is different from memorizing your presentation, which is always a bad idea (see chapter 4). The mental walk-through familiarizes you with the flow of the presentation. Do this exercise until you become familiar with all parts of your presentation. Then do it some more.

1. Walk through each step of your presentation.

2. Imagine your successful introduction of each step and point.

3. Go through TO THE END each time. Repeat.

Use 3x5 Cards

Write down three to seven key phrases on each 3x5 card. Organize the cards in the chronology of your presentation. The cards work as a way to remind you of key phrases and provide you with a place to record ideas, transitions, and other material that will make your flow of words seem natural and relaxed. Just the act of writing these cards will go a long way toward putting these phrases and points in your head.

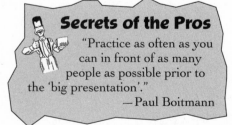

Secrets of the Pros

"Practice as often as you can in front of as many people as possible prior to the 'big presentation'."

—Paul Boitmann

Once you've rehearsed with the 3x5 cards a few times something magical begins to happen; you begin to form a mental picture of the cards. In a best case scenario, you'll carry a mental image of these cards into your presentation. But even if you don't, you

31

can carry the actual cards—they're small, they're something you rehearsed with, and they make great inconspicuous notes. Remember to number your cards in case they are dropped.

Practice in Front of Someone—and, if Possible, Use Video!

Obvious? Maybe. But for some mysterious reason most people—and highly experienced speakers and presenters are sometimes the worst culprits—fail to take this crucial step. You must practice out loud in front of people. Remember: what sounds good on paper (and even in your head) doesn't always work in front of an audience. Any problem with your presentation is simple enough to fix when a friend, spouse, or coworker catches it three days before you're on.

> **Secrets of the Pros**
>
> "... success: Everybody talks about it, but far too many people do little or nothing to insure their own personal success."
> —Paul J. Meyer

Practicing in front of people also gets you through the mechanics of moving from mental rehearsal to physical rehearsal. A lot can happen to a word as it travels from your brain to your mouth. It's best to have any mishaps occur on the testing grounds and not on the race-track!

Another trick: videotape yourself—over and over. There's no replacement for understanding how you look when speaking. Watch the tape to see:

➤ How well do the words and transitions flow?

➤ How comfortable do you appear with the material?

➤ How is your posture, pronunciation, and word speed?

➤ How can you make it all *better?*

Practice Makes Perfect

Your face is one of your most important instruments as a presenter. Become familiar with it and practice using it the way musicians practice with their instruments. Use the mirror regularly! Some tips to practice in front of a mirror:

➤ Get to know what your face really looks like.

➤ Practice smiling naturally.

➤ Know how your expression appears when you are: happy, angry, nervous, tired, etc.

Rehearse with the Equipment You Will Be Using

When rehearsing, do so with the equipment you intend to use. (For an in-depth discussion of the presentation tools you may use and how to use them, turn to chapter 10.) If you'll be using flip charts, practice with flip charts. If you'll be using videotape and overheads, rehearse with them. Equipment can cause mechanical and logistical headaches. You ought to get used to the mechanics of using them in the right way and at the right time ahead of schedule. Actors do dress rehearsals—so should you!

The Last Hours Before Your Presentation

There's no replacement for rehearsing in the actual room. If that's not practical, rehearse in a similar room or set up a room in your house as nearly as possible to your presentation room. Always try to GET INTO THE ACTUAL ROOM to get acclimated before the presentation.

There are two reasons to do this. First, you need to physically know the space. Where are the light switches, outlets, doors, tables, chairs, any cords or rough spots in the rug that might make you fall flat on your face (figuratively AND literally). Equally important, is the idea that you must make the room mentally yours. At this stage of the game, you're close to being fully prepared. Drive home your preparation by walking through the room. Know every corner of it from a presenter's perspective.

Secrets of the Pros

"Winners are those people who make a habit of doing the things losers are uncomfortable doing."
—Ed Foreman

Finally, do something few presenters ever do. SIT IN YOUR AUDIENCE'S SEATS! Know how the room looks and feels to them. Can everyone see well from every seat? Can they hear audio equipment? Can they see the front of the room? Do they have enough room to be comfortable? It's a good idea to do this, because in a few short hours, the audience will become the most important people in your life. Know how they feel by literally sitting in their seats.

Developing Your Presentation

CHECKLIST FOR EFFECTIVE REHEARSAL

Well before your presentation:

Prepare and mentally walk-through:

❑ 3-D outline

❑ Each section of presentation

❑ 3x5 cards

Rehearse in front of :

❑ Other people

❑ Video camera

❑ Mirror

Just before your presentation:

Locate and know how to operate
the following fixtures:

❑ Electrical outlets

❑ Lighting controls

❑ Volume controls for room sound

❑ Window-blind cords

Locate the following:

❑ Restrooms

❑ Telephones

❑ Stairs and elevators

❑ Smoking areas

Comments:

_____

_____

_____

_____

_____

_____

_____

_____

Very Important Points to Remember

✔ Begin developing your presentation with a clear idea of your limitations and then fill out a "presentation work order" to develop realistic expectations.

✔ Create a three-dimensional outline to really know where you're going.

✔ Logically order the material of your presentation by mixing and matching sequences in your presentation's subsections.

✔ The most important three steps to take for an effective presentation:

➤ Rehearse

➤ Rehearse

➤ Rehearse

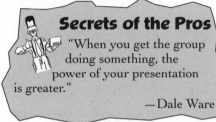

Secrets of the Pros

"When you get the group doing something, the power of your presentation is greater."

—Dale Ware

✔ Always take time to sit in your audience's seats as part of your rehearsal. Knowing how the world looks to them makes you a superior presenter.

Fill in Your Favorite Tips from the Chapter

✔ _____

_____

✔ _____

_____

✔ _____

_____

✔ _____

_____

Developing Your Presentation

This chapter reveals:

➤ Proven methods for calming the jitters
➤ Proven methods for getting in a confident state of mind
➤ Tips on how to bond with your audience
➤ Tips on how to make enthusiasm rise from the ashes of your nervousness

3

Nervous to Natural

Nervous to Natural

JEARY THEORY

Nervousness comes from the fear of the unknown. Clarify the sources of your nervousness and you can conquer it.

"It all changed when I realized I'm not the only one on the planet who's scared. Everyone else is too."

—Stan Dale

Secret Steps for Going from Nervous to Natural

1. **Know what you're talking about.**

   Thorough preparation equals total confidence. Prepare then rehearse, rehearse, rehearse! Understand that your audience really wants you to succeed.

   Practice meaningfully—the way you'll actually deliver your presentation. Refer to chapter 2 for the best techniques on rehearsing.

2. **Be yourself.**

   Use your own natural speaking style. Don't try to be someone you're not.

Secrets of the Pros

"A man's doubts and fears are his worst enemies."
—William Wrigley, Jr.

3. Psyche yourself up—use positive self-talk.

Visualize success: picture your audience applauding you at the end of your presentation then work toward it.

4. Work with your body's physical reaction to nerves.

Do stretching, isometrics, or some other exercise to relieve physical nervousness.

Take deep breaths to control breathing.

Pausing: proper pausing conveys relaxation and confidence.

5. Bond with your audience.

Keep the audience on your side.

Pick two or three friendly faces; speak to them in your opening and feed off their positive energy.

Get a good night's sleep before your presentation.

The Scene . . .

You know you have to lead a presentation at the quarterly sales meeting next month and you know your material well—your boss knows that. But you're terrified of speaking in front of people.

Or—you've prepared and rehearsed for your presentation on local safety issues to be delivered to the local Commerce Committee until it seems like you could deliver it in your sleep. Your 3-D outline is as solid as Plymouth Rock. You look great on your videotape. But as soon as you stand up to rehearse in front of two or three of your friends, your mind goes blank. You have to look at your rehearsal cards, which confuses you even more, and before you know it, it's as if you never even prepared. If you can't stay calm in front of three or four friends, how will you ever manage to deliver your presentation in front of a room full of strangers?

Or—in about one hour you have to speak You've been reviewing your notes, avoiding coffee, and trying to psyche yourself up for success. But you're so nervous that

> **Secrets of the Pros**
>
> "Do what you know, what you live, what you believe. Doing overcomes fear every time!"
>
> —Ed Foreman

your hands are shaking and your knees feel weak. If only there were something to do to get it under control

The Solution . . .

Since there's more than one kind of nervousness (as the previous scenes suggest), we need a system that addresses all the different ways in which we feel nervous, a single system that addresses the physical manifestations of nervousness—butterflies in the stomach, dry mouth, wet palms—as well as the mental manifestations— negative self-talk, fear, and apprehension. In fact, an ideal solution would take all that energy you're wasting on being nervous and funnel it back into the presentation in the form of enthusiasm.

> ### Secrets of the Pros
> "Everyone has butterflies in their stomach. The only difference between a pro and an amateur is: the pro has the butterflies in formation!"
> —Zig Ziglar

You're Not Alone

There's good news and bad news about nervousness—the good news is that everyone feels it. The bad news is that everyone feels it. Or more accurately, it never goes away. The differences between those who appear to be free of nervousness and those who suffer the devastating effects of obvious nervousness at the front of the room is *control*. Every time you see someone who seems relaxed, confident, and natural at the front of the room, it's because that person has mastered the techniques of keeping her nervousness under control so well that she'll never let you see her sweat!

Speaking in public is the number-one fear of people in America— if you can conquer this, it gives you a great competitive edge!

Step 1. Conquer Nervousness: Know What You're Talking About

The single best way to fight nerves is to prepare yourself. This is because nervousness is rooted in psychological stress (fear of failure) that manifests itself in physical symptoms (fast pulse, shallow breathing, dry mouth, sweaty palms, sick stomach, strange

voice, and jittery knees).
The bottom line is: preparation pays big dividends.
If you've prepared well
and still feel nervous, your
preparation is going to
help reduce your nerves
once you begin to talk.

This section of the book
and its tips deals with
nerves at all stages of the
game—a month before,
the night before, or the
hour before your presentation. If you've followed
the easy steps to preparation and rehearsal outlined in chapters 1
and 2, you've probably got a whole binder full of papers. The night
before your presentation, TAKE ACTION by reviewing these
notes and running the checklists you've prepared. This action will
help reduce nerves.

> ### Top Ten Fears Among Americans
> 1. Speaking before a group
> 2. Heights
> 3. Insects and bugs
> 4. Financial problems
> 5. Deep water
> 6. Sickness
> 7. DEATH (!!!)
> *8. Flying
> 9. Loneliness
> 10. Dogs
>
> From *The Book of Lists*

Professional speaker David Peoples, author of *Presentations Plus*,
has this to say about reducing nervousness:

> "The single most effective thing you can do for sweaty
> palms is *rehearse*. The second most effective thing you
> can do for sweaty palms is *rehearse*. Guess what the third
> most effective thing is?"

Knowing that you have done your homework and are well prepared will provide you with a peaceful confidence that will kick-in soon after you get a few words out of your mouth. You can jumpstart this process by getting the audience involved quickly.

Thorough preparation equals total confidence. Prepare then rehearse, rehearse, rehearse! Understand that your audience really wants you to succeed!

Step 2: Be Yourself

Don't even think about trying to be someone you're not. You might see a great presenter a week before your presentation—someone who has a Don Rickles style of poking jokes at the audience, or someone who runs back and forth and makes things up as she goes along. The audience may love these folks and you might be tempted to imitate them. Take it from me—don't.

Audiences see through pretense. You have enough to worry about when you're giving a presenta-tion—don't add to your burden by trying to do imitations. Here's just a partial list of what can go wrong when you try to be someone else.

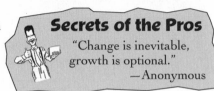

Secrets of the Pros

"Change is inevitable, growth is optional."
—Anonymous

➤ You can make a poor first impression and then have nowhere to fall back.

➤ Humor will be strained, because it is not natural—not from your heart, like all good humor. Unnatural humor ranges from dry and boring to utterly disastrous.

➤ Your eye contact will be weak because you'll be busy focusing on being something you're not.

➤ You will invariably lack conviction and enthusiasm.

➤ The audience will resent your attempt or be embarrassed for you.

All of which is to say once more: Be yourself!

"What if my natural self is a nervous wreck?" you ask. Great question! Proceed to step three and let's get to work fixing up that nervous wreck.

The Only Time to Be Something Other than Yourself

Acting confident and enthusiastic actually helps to bring on confi-dence and enthusiasm. If you are passionate about what you are presenting and believe in what you're doing, it will be easy for you to deal with your nerves when you follow the tips in this book. Don't imitate actions or habits of other speakers—imitate only their confidence by emulating their preparation.

Being Yourself Can Be Humorous

Professional facilitator Myra Ketterman tells a story about her seventeen-year-old son, Jared, with whom she has a very close relationship. One day when Myra left home, she called back wanting to chat with Jared one more time before hopping on the plane. Jared answered the phone with his usual sweet southern "Hello," and Myra said, "Jared, I sure do love you." Jared replied, "Hey, I love you too! Who is this?" He was a bit surprised to discover it was Mom and there was definitely follow-up to that conversation!

Everyone in her audience relates to the humor in her story. Many are parents of teenagers, or at least they can remember being seventeen themselves. It's another great way to break the ice and move into feeling more natural.

Step 3: Psyche Yourself Up Effectively: Your Mind's Reaction

Everyone speaks to him or herself. It may or may not be in words—but in any case you give yourself messages and commands constantly. In fact, we do it so often, we don't even think about it. This constant, often wordless, dialogue we carry on with ourselves is known in the presentation business as "self-talk." All too often we let our self-talk become negative without realizing it. Often, it's the most common of phrases. Some examples of this include:

➤ "They're gonna hate me."

➤ "I'll never get prepared in time."

➤ "I'm just too nervous to stand up in front of those people."

➤ "Last time I stood up in front of this group, I dropped all my files—what if it happens again?"

This negative self-talk sends exactly the wrong message to our-selves—it psyches us out. Change this negative self-talk! Try something positive:

➤ The audience is going to love me because *they really want me to succeed.* (See sidebar on facing page.)

➤ If I take a deep breath and concentrate, I will be *more than prepared* on time.

➤ Following the steps to reducing nerves in *Inspire Any Audience: Proven Secrets of the Pros* will make me confident and competent in front of ANY audience. All I have to do is be myself.

> **Visualize success: picture your audience applauding you at the end of your presentation, then work toward that goal.**

➤ Last time I stood up in front of this group, I dropped my files — but I also got them laughing *with* me at the end of my presentation. I'll focus on the positive outcome, not a negative incident.

If you can't help but think negatively, try this. Visualize failure and then raving success. Which is more fun? A technique I've used to calm my jitters is to put things into perspective. I "catastrophize" and ask myself, "What's the worst possible thing that can happen?" In the big scheme of things, the worst possible thing to happen during my presentation probably isn't that terrible anyway. It is only a blip on the radar scope of eternity. Think positively!

FACT: Your Audience Really Wants You to Succeed

Think back to the last time you were at a circus or saw one on TV. Imagine now you are in that audience at the circus and far above you the trapeze artists are working their magic, with the greatest of ease. Fun, right? Now the trick gets harder as the trapeze artist's crew removes the net from beneath her. You tense up, maybe sit on the edge of your seat, and glance at the people around you. In short, you're nervous as heck. The stunt proceeds and the daring young lady flies from her bar out into empty air. The audience gasps, and then her partner, from nowhere, swoops into the picture and snags her back to safety — and everyone breathes a sigh of relief.

Why? Because deep down we want her to succeed. *Your* audience is the same. For the most part, they are nearly as anxious as you. Always remind yourself of this simple but powerful fact: *my audience wants me to succeed*. This is true of even a fairly hostile audience, and is probably due to the fact that we have an inborn tendency to enjoy the spectacle of success. We all love success!

The Mind-Body Connection

Self-talk works for you (or against you) because of what nervousness really is. What we call nervousness is really our body's natural response to stressful situations.

Scientists believe that these feelings date back to our prehistoric ancestors, who were instinctively programmed for "fight or flight" when faced with stress in the wild — maybe in the form of a sabertoothed tiger or a big brown bear.

Secrets of the Pros

"The human mind is a wonderful thing — it starts working the minute you're born and never stops until you get up to speak in public."
— Roscoe Drummond

Today, when we're faced with the unknown — such as speaking in front of a group of people we don't know — that old mechanism kicks in and our body gets prepared for fight or flight. Modern civilized life doesn't leave us much room for fighting.

As a result, we have nowhere to turn to relieve this stress. Our ancestors could burn away this stress by defending themselves or hightailing it out of there. But we have to bottle it up and stand there. That internalized energy causes all those unpleasant physical sensations we call nerves, platform jitters, the shakes, and so on.

Step 4. Learn to Work with Your Body's Physical Reaction

Positive thinking won't make the symptoms of nervousness disappear altogether, though it will greatly reduce your body's tendency to get nervous. And sometimes, as I mentioned above, your body can be treacherous. Even though you know better, even though you think positively, your body insists on going through the motions of feeling nervous. Unfortunately, the appearance of nervousness is often more than enough to cause the reality of nervousness.

Fortunately, once you know a handful of "secret" techniques, dealing with nervousness is far easier than you might imagine. The key to gaining control of your body's reaction to the fight-or-flight instinct is to

Fear: A distressing emotion aroused by an impending pain, danger, or evil; or by the illusion of such.

understand that the symptoms of nervousness come from the tension of not being able to burn off the fight-or-flight adrenaline. Burn off the excess energy, relax, and you reduce the nerves.

Physical stress reducers:
- ➤ Deep breathing
- ➤ Isometric exercises
- ➤ Vigorous exercises
- ➤ Relaxation techniques
- ➤ Yawning
- ➤ Talking to yourself
- ➤ Moving and gesturing
- ➤ Pausing

Deep breathing helps control stress by returning our breathing to its natural, pre-stress patterns. Try taking a few deep breaths then attempt to breathe normally over a period of a few minutes.

Isometric exercises are stationary exercises in which one group of muscles works against another. Try pressing your fingertips gently together, then press harder and hold for a few seconds. You can even do these as you begin speaking—no one will know that you're burning bottled stress and reducing nervousness.

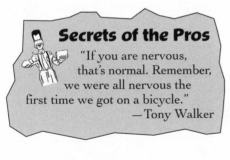

Secrets of the Pros

"If you are nervous, that's normal. Remember, we were all nervous the first time we got on a bicycle."
—Tony Walker

Vigorous exercises such as jogging, walking, or swimming help keep stress low. A night or two before your presentation, take time out to go for a walk. If you're still nervous just before your presentation, find a storage room or empty rest room and do a few vigorous jumping jacks. Don't drench yourself in sweat, just do enough to get the blood flowing. It's a great stress reducer.

Relaxation techniques: Relax by focusing on tense muscle groups. First relax your scalp, then your eyebrows and ears, then your tongue and jaw, then shoulders and on down to your feet. Repeat as necessary or try stretching in combination with this technique.

Yawning is the natural way to relax. Try yawning widely a few times. It's the body's natural way of relaxing itself. It also stretches the muscles of your neck and throat to make for more natural speaking.

Talking to yourself: This is different from self-talking. Here I mean *literally* talk to yourself to warm up your voice. One trick: practice saying "Good morning!" over and over as you're on your way to a presentation. People may look at you as if you're nuts, but it's a small price to pay to reduce nerves and get yourself prepared for a great presentation!

Moving and gesturing: As you begin to speak, move, gesture, and burn some nervous energy. It catches your audience's attention when you're animated.

Pausing: Once you begin speaking, nerves can make you speak quickly, alerting everyone to your nervous state. Control it by learning to pause. Proper pausing conveys relaxation and confidence. An audience will sit up and listen when you pause. Surprisingly a pause of two, three, or even more seconds not only catches the attention of the audience, it lets them know you're in command. Learn to use the power of silence!

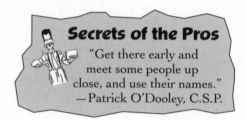

Secrets of the Pros

"Get there early and meet some people up close, and use their names."
—Patrick O'Dooley, C.S.P.

Practice one or more of these techniques regularly and learn how to tailor them to your own particular patterns of nervousness. Combined with positive self-talk they represent a powerful combination for combating nervousness.

Step 5: Bonding with the Audience

Don't be too concerned if you still have a touch of nervous energy left as you approach the front of the room. It's useful energy at this point—in fact, it's something you can use to build excitement, project enthusiasm, and create a bond with the audience. Building an early rapport helps boost your confidence and increases the audience's natural urge to want you to succeed.

Bonding with your audience begins long before you start to speak.

➤ **Arrive early**—before any audience members do. This sends the message that you care enough to get things ready in advance.

➤ **Meet and greet the audience yourself**—I never cease to be amazed at presenters who stand off in one corner or officiously read notes while their audience files in. Get on your feet and greet! This gives you a great opportunity to build rapport by meeting audience members as individuals. Always ask for their names, shake their hands, and make solid eye contact. When there's time, finding out how far they drove to get to the presentation, where they work, and other personal information provides you with important material and begins the process of developing audience advocates.

➤ **Start off by grabbing your audience's attention**—(See chapter 4, "The First Three Minutes," for details.) Get your audience involved immediately! This will make them buy-in to what you say for the rest of your presentation.

➤ **Let your audience know what's in it for them**—Begin with a statement that reduces their nervousness. (Yes, your audience is nervous, like you—everyone is!) Let them know they aren't wasting their time.

➤ **Make eye contact**—Search out a few friendly faces—those folks who are smiling, nodding at what you say, laughing at your jokes. Look them in the eye and draw power from them. A good place to start are those few brave souls who sat in the front seats.

Reducing Nervousness

Your audience is almost as nervous as you are. Get them participating as soon as possible to calm everyone's nerves. One icebreaker you might try is to have everyone share his/her favorite hobby, quote, or a bit of background information about themselves. This is usually a winner that lets people have fun and helps to get your butterflies flying in formation.

Gwyn and Tony prepare name tags.

➤ **Show genuine enthusiasm** — Let them know you're happy to be there, and they will be too. This will reduce your nervousness and make you comfortable.

You probably didn't know all or even most of this information beforehand. Chances are no one told you that learning these things can make a friend of your audience. Getting that information before- hand greatly increases your success rate and confidence, thereby reducing or even eliminating your nervousness. You might have heard how important it is to "build a rapport" with your audience — that is, getting them to know and like you. But has anyone ever told you that building a rapport with your audience begins BEFORE you ever see them? The research you do even just a day or two before you meet your audience can make a big difference. They will begin to know and like you at the beginning of the talk if you have begun to know (and like) them BEFORE the talk.

> **Secrets of the Pros**
>
> "We tend to get what we expect."
> — Norman Vincent Peale

Bond with Your Audience

When you stand up to talk to your children (or friends or relatives), do you feel nervous? In most situations, probably not. Why? Because you know them. What makes other audiences scary is that we simply have too little information on them.

Think of the last group you spoke to. Did you know?

➤ Their names?

➤ Why they were in the room with you?

➤ What they expected to get from listening to you?

➤ What was in your talk for them?

➤ Their likes and dislikes?

➤ The level of knowledge they brought to your discussion?

➤ How to pronounce their names individually?

➤ What kinds of presentation have worked for this group or one like it in the past?

➤ Do they like jokes? What kind?

One More Note on Nerves

Nervousness doesn't have to be your enemy. It's a natural and healthy sign. The day I stop feeling nervous is the day I know I'm no longer an effective presenter. The trick to nerves is making them work for you and not against you. Always strive to appear poised. It's one of the few miracles of the real world. The more you practice not *looking* nervous, the more you become *less* nervous. And finally, never apologize to your audience for feeling nervous. Your audience has no idea you're feeling the jitters. Only you can let them know, so don't!

Very Important Points to Remember

✔ Everyone gets nervous — it's a natural physical reaction that can be controlled, both mentally and physically.

Tony gets to know audience members prior to a presentation, while John double-checks the order of the overheads.

✔ Your audience really *wants* you to win.

✔ Being completely prepared is the key to reducing nervousness.

✔ Use positive self-talk to reduce your mental stress.

✔ Use appropriate stress and tension reduction exercises to lessen your physical stress.

✔ Convert nervousness to enthusiasm by bonding with your audience. Get them immediately involved.

✔ Practice feeling confident and you will be confident. Never let 'em see you sweat!

Fill in Your Favorite Tips from the Chapter

✔ _____

_____

✔ _____

_____

✔ _____

_____

✔ _____

_____

PART 2
Beginning Your Presentation

This chapter reveals:

➤ How to get off to a great start by building rapport and earning respect
➤ A collection of audience-grabbing openers
➤ What the "Four Audience-Tensions" are and how to alleviate them

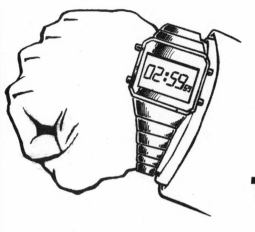

The First Three Minutes

"You are an unknown quantity for only 120 seconds.
After that everything you say will be heard in the con-
text of the impression from your first two minutes."

—David Peoples,
Presentations Plus

The Scene...

This is it! You've prepared, you've rehearsed, you've got your nervousness under strict control, and now you're ready for the big
time. You're delivering a presentation at the annual convention to
a group of one hundred fifty knowledgeable professionals from
around the country. You've been at the front of the room before,
and you know that beginning a presentation is a little like piloting
an airplane—take-off is the most critical phase. If they don't buy-in
now, you'll be playing catch-up all week. What you need is a surefire tool for the first three minutes so that you can grab the audience's attention.

53

The Solution . . .

Is a system to build rapport with your audience, grab their attention, and make them buy-in to what you're saying immediately. The first three minutes are different from the rest of your presentation for the following reasons:

➤ Your audience's attention is naturally high.

➤ Most audiences spend the first 180 seconds of any presentation sizing up the presenter.

➤ You've got just one chance to make a first impression.

➤ First impressions are lasting impressions and are, therefore, a speaker's best opportunity to win an audience over.

Know the secrets to a great first three minutes.

Secrets

1. **Show respect and build rapport.**

   ➤ Make the audience your partner.

   ➤ Prove you respect their time.

   ➤ Prove you're prepared.

   ➤ Empathize with your audience and communicate similar interests. (Show commonality—people like people who are like themselves.)

   ➤ Use eye contact—it's an attention-grabber.

2. **Grab the audience's attention and run with it.**

   ➤ The hook

   ➤ Use an attention-grabber (an immediate benefit or concurrence for/from the audience).

   ➤ Know and use the different types of openers:

   • Current event

   • Humorous

   • Pictorial

   • Anecdotal

   • Pertinent quote

   • Real-world situation

- Rhetorical
- Musical

➤ There are four sure ways to KILL an opening:
- An apology
- An unrelated or inappropriate anecdote
- Long- or slow-moving statements
- Equipment failure

➤ "Must-Dos" in the first three minutes:
1. Focus wandering minds to topic at hand.
2. Use appropriate words and gestures.
3. Get audience commitment to stay involved.

Step 1. Show Respect and Build Rapport

In the preceding chapter, we discussed the fact that most audiences want the speaker to succeed. Even negative folks have a vested interest in your success. The more successful you are, the more enjoyable your presentation will be, even for them. There are three things every audience loves:

1. Respect (for their time, their dignity, their feelings, etc.)
2. Rapport (between the speaker and themselves)
3. Entertainment

Who knows . . . above and beyond these three things, your audience may actually enjoy the message of your presentation! Kidding aside, these three elements provide a threshold for audience buy-in, involvement, and satisfaction. The first words out of your mouth should carry your audience over this threshold and prove that you will, above all else, deliver these three audience imperatives.

Why the First Three Minutes?

In the first three minutes of your presentation, your audience is sizing you up. They're deciding whether they like you and you like them, and they're wondering whether or not you're worth listening to. Grab them early, and they'll stick by you even if something goes wrong later; lose them, and, at best, you're playing catch-up for the rest of your presentation.

Make the Audience Your Partner

The way to guarantee an audience's commitment and loyalty to you is to immediately involve them in your presentation! There's an old saying: "Nobody believes they have an ugly baby," so the key to audience buy-in (a prerequisite for audience inspiration) is to make them part-owner of the presentation — make the presentation half *their* baby! Once your audience has taken partial ownership of the presentation, you are destined for success, because your audience will not let you fail. There are three steps in making the audience your partner:

Secrets of the Pros

"I first try to get them to move forward. Then I remind myself that the ones who did show up deserve the best that I've got and I try to give it to them."

—Jeff Slutsky, Streetfighter Marketing

1. Meet as many attendees as possible *before* the presentation. This begins to build a one-on-one bond that will carry over into the first few minutes of your presentation.

2. Prove you respect them by starting the presentation on time.

3. Ask them what their own expectations are.

Step three deserves special attention. Asking the audience to provide their own expectations gives them a feeling of input and control and lets them know you care about their feelings. You can write their expectations on a flip chart, let them know what expectations you can reasonably meet and what ones you cannot, and then use that page again later to prove you've delivered value.

Prove That You Respect Their Time

You've put a lot of effort into preparing your presentation. Hours, days, maybe weeks. Why? Because you care about your audience and respect their time. Unfortunately, audiences have no way of knowing this UNLESS YOU TELL THEM. An audience expects the room to be set up, the speaker to be well-prepared and well-groomed, and all manner of things to be in order when they arrive — so it doesn't always occur to them how much time and preparation went into getting ready.

At some point in your first three minutes let them know that because you respect their time, hours and hours of preparation went into the presentation. Let the audience know that your respect for their valuable time will continue through the rest of the presentation.

Prove That You're Prepared

Nothing sends the signal that you don't care like being unprepared. Every detail counts. Starting on time, having the appropriate materials ready, knowing what you're going to say. The audience notices everything when it comes to preparation. If they get the feeling that you are ill-prepared, they'll tune out. In order to better demonstrate preparedness, make sure you're prepared with the answers to some questions that will be important to them. Such questions might include:

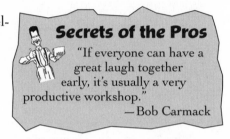

Secrets of the Pros

"If everyone can have a great laugh together early, it's usually a very productive workshop."
—Bob Carmack

➤ Who are you?

➤ How long is the day scheduled to run?

➤ How frequently will breaks be taken?

➤ What can I gain from your presentation?

➤ Where are the rest rooms, telephones, and smoking areas?

Use Eye Contact

Nothing builds rapport faster than eye contact. Think of all the clichés that reference the power of eye contact. We don't believe a word from the "shifty-eyed salesman;" we can't trust someone

First Impressions

Audiences gain their first impressions of a speaker from four areas:

➤ Appearance—Dress and grooming

➤ Orderliness—Room set-up, materials

➤ Qualities as a Host—Making audiences comfortable

➤ Credibility—Knowledge of subject and speaking ability.

—Doug Kevorkian

who's afraid to "look you in the eye"; the eyes are the "windows to the soul;" and we "eye something suspiciously" if we don't trust it.

Start off your first three minutes by making solid eye contact with at least a few members of the audience. Don't scan the audience—speak *to* individual participants and make eye contact while doing it. Even those members of the audience that you're not making eye contact with will benefit, because they will be able to see that you *are* talking to individuals. In addition to creating the impression that you are confident and honest, eye contact keeps your audience alert and communicates your interest in them.

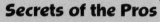

Secrets of the Pros

"I always strive to get the audience into the subject as quickly as possible. Many times, my first statement is a question looking for a response. This is a tremendous icebreaker."
—Paul Boitmann

The Twelve Commandments

Building rapport is critical for achieving audience buy-in—and without 100 percent buy-in, it's terribly difficult to inspire an audience to act. In fact, audience rapport is so important that I've coined the Twelve Commandments to follow when building rapport.

The Twelve Commandments of Building and Maintaining Rapport

1. Thou shalt respect thy audience.

2. Whenever possible thou shalt meet with members of thy audience *before* thy talk . . . shake their hands, ask their names, and begin to know them as individual people. This will create an early bond that can last throughout the talk.

3. Thou shalt start on time.

4. When possible thou shalt bestow small presents upon thy audience members.

5. Thou shalt maintain good individual eye contact: avoid scanning thy audience.

6. Thou shalt attempt to learn and use some of thy audience's own buzz words, acronyms, and jargon whenever possible and, of course, acknowledge participants by name.

7. Thou shalt convey apprecia-
tion—nothing connects two
people better than a sincere
compliment.

8. Thou shalt use breaks to
continue nurturing rapport;
socialize with thy audience!

9. Thou shalt seek feedback,
especially on things that
affect audience comfort:
room temperature, volume-
level, speed of thy talk, etc.

> **Eye contact**
> The eyes don't lie. If the
> first words out of your
> mouth are, "I'm thrilled to
> be here," but you're staring
> at the floor in front of your
> feet, your audience will
> learn not to trust a word
> you say. Definitely *not* a
> favorable first impression.

10. Thou shalt praise audience members and maketh them heroes.

11. Thou shalt learn to be a good listener: give good eye contact,
pause, listen to the entire statement, and nary make a joke about
a participant comment.

12. Thou shalt mirror thy audience's speaking patterns—if they talk
fast, talk fast; if they speak slowly, slow down.

STEP 2. Grab the Audience's Attention

The Hook

How many times have you
heard a speaker start with
this line: "Good morning
(afternoon, evening), ladies
and gentlemen"? Dozens?
Hundreds? It's the most
tired line in any speaker's
repertoire, yet speakers and
presenters return to it time
and again. It's comfortable,
expected, and BORING!
Rather than starting off with
a line no one hears (it's the
speaking equivalent of asking, "How are you?"), try to

Tony introduces Roger Clarke, who helped set up the event.

open with a line that grabs the
audience's attention. The line
doesn't have to be outrageous,
just interesting. It should also
be something that gets the
audience involved at some
level—even it is only to raise
their hands or answer a
question.

Secrets of the Pros

"Remember to show the
audience that you are
human. Let them know
that you have the same desires,
challenges and stresses that they
have. This may be your greatest
source of credibility."
—Sherry Boecher

Hooks

Anything that grabs the audience's attention and makes them listen
functions as a hook. Of course, some work better than others. Here
are a few surefire ways to make your audience listen:

➤ Start with a startling statistic. "Nearly everyone in this room
   has passed up an opportunity to become a millionaire."

➤ Start with a proactive question. "How many of you in this room
   have bought a foreign-made product this week?"

➤ Tell a story about something that recently happened to you.

➤ Refer to some current newsworthy event. Make sure it applies
   to the subject at hand.

Use hooks to signal that you're different from other presenters that
your audience may have seen, many of whom might have begun
with clunkers like these:

➤ "Good morning, ladies and gentlemen."

➤ "Let's review some administrative details."

➤ "I'm not much of a speaker, but here goes . . ."

Below is a list of openers that grab an audience's attention and get
them involved.

Know Your Openers!

Current Event: People are interested in current events. Open
with a comment on some local or national event that will get them
interested. Especially useful are human interest, new findings, car
and home prices, and local events. Avoid politics, religion, and
other controversial topics.

Humor: Start with a funny story, observation, or activity. Make sure it is somehow pertinent to the topic at hand or illustrates some point you wish the audience to understand. Laughing gets the audience on your side! As a rule, avoid jokes. They sound canned, usually have nothing to do with the topic, and seem to always offend someone.

Use an anecdote: Another way to use storytelling is to tell an anecdote that illustrates some important concept that your talk deals with. The key to using anecdotes is to keep them short and to the point. Better to tell a short story and leave the audience wanting more than to draw a story out and bore them.

Use a quotation: Quotations are often filled with wisdom, carry authority, and can sometimes make a point more clearly than we can. Use them. Books packed with good quotes from different people on hundreds of subjects can be found in the reference section of any library or bookstore.

Create a real-world situation: A recognizable scene grabs attention (see the beginning of each chapter in this book). Audiences respond to "seeing themselves" in a situation.

Ask a question: Questions are great because they require an answer. Ask something provocative and a little mysterious about the audience: "How many of you have a remote-control television at home?" Then tie the question to a point you wish to make.

Trivia, statistics, little-known facts: Did you know that a person's heart pumps one million times in an average lifetime? That the average lightning bolt has enough energy to light up a city? That more Americans are injured in auto accidents each year than were injured in all of our wars combined? Neither does your audience. Using appropriate facts and trivia affects your audience like a jolt of adrenaline.

Play some music: Music is powerful stuff—it will awaken the audience and you can often use it to make a point. Go for high-energy, upbeat music when you want to crank up audience energy.

Give something away: People love free stuff. Give something away and your audience will get a big kick out of it. Even the smallest trinkets can serve as a memento for your presentation.

Giving Something Away

Probably my biggest trademark as a presenter is giving away dollar bills. You read correctly. I have a pad of brand-new, mint dollar bills put on a cardboard backing with a gummy spine. I give them to

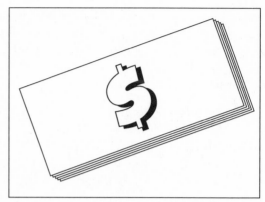

audience members. I use them in the first three minutes to get the room laughing and warmed up—then throughout the day I give them away for funny comments, for special help, and so on. It's always a hit and well worth the few dollars it costs me.

Five Sure Ways to Kill Your Opening

There are plenty of good ways to open your presentation effectively. And there are five sure ways to ruin your opening. Whatever else you do in your first three minutes, DO NOT do the following:

1. **Never start late.** This sends the signal that everything you say is subject to change. Pick a starting time and stick with it.

2. **Never start with an apology.** Don't apologize for anything. If it's a big mistake, your audience will see it and, believe me, they'll know you're sorry. If it's a small mistake, they won't notice it unless you bring it to their attention by apologizing. And never start a story or comical anecdote with an apologetic disclaimer like "I'm not much of a comedian, but here goes . . ." Doing so sets you up for failure. Always think positively.

> **Secrets of the Pros**
>
> "Words have power. Words have altered the course of history and changed forever the destiny of individuals who spoke out."
>
> —Terrence J. McCann, Executive Director, Toastmasters International

3. **Never start with an unrelated or inappropriate anecdote.** A presentation has to be *about* something. If your stories or anecdotes are unrelated to the topic, they will confuse your audience.

Quotations

Quotations are great for a number of reasons. They have built-in brevity—part of what makes a quotation work is that it is short and to-the-point. Quotations usually contain an element of essential truth, the I-know-exactly-what-you-mean quality that delights readers and listeners. Many have withstood the test of time, dating back thousands of years.

When using quotations, follow these few simple rules.

1. Make sure the quote reinforces your message.

2. Include some background information to make the quote meaningful. Henry Ford will require a little less background than Thucydides.

3. Make sure it is related: avoid being a showoff. Too many quotes or quotes from obscure sources may give the impression that you *think* you know a lot. It's okay to be smart. But rubbing your audience's face in your knowledge is the surest way to turn them off.

4. Quote correctly. Misquoting can kill your credibility, especially if someone in your audience points out you've misquoted. Always write out any quotation you're using word for word. When in doubt, paraphrase. Make sure you pronounce the name of your source correctly.

Never use a racy anecdote in front of an audience. The dividends from a good anecdote and a laugh are great but never great enough to risk alienating even a few of your audience members with an offensive remark.

4. **Never start slowly**. Open with a bang and *move*. Always stay a step ahead of the audience. This doesn't mean talk fast; it means don't dawdle when telling stories or making points. Avoid opening with boring material such as administrative matters. Save that sort of thing for the middle section of your speech and even then, keep it brief.

5. **Never start with equipment failure**. No matter how well you've prepared, if your microphone fails, if your VCR monitor isn't ready or the light bulb on your overhead projector is burned out you'll look ill-prepared. If something breaks while you're using it

Music

I was sitting on a panel to select presenters auditioning for a multimillion-dollar training program. It's hard to imagine a presenting situation more stressful than *presenting* to get a job. Speaker Fred Collins was one of the auditioners. He approached the front of the room with a winning smile on his face, carrying a portable tape deck—a miniature boom-box. He set the tape player on a table near the front of the room, touched the PLAY button and the song "I Feel Good!" blasted out. Even the most important of the important people in the room couldn't help smiling and feeling good! In twenty seconds Fred Collins built rapport with a tough audience, won them over, and landed himself a good job in the process!

NEVER stop to repair it. Acknowledge the problem, then move along. Audiences understand that accidents happen; what they don't understand is having to wait for you to fix something. Better to skip something than make your audience wait for a troubleshooter to come in and fix a broken piece of equipment!

Make Sure Your Body Reinforces What You Say

A few years ago some researchers at UCLA conducted a study that has become famous in the presentation world. In it they found that the success of a public presentation depends about 7 percent on the words that are actually spoken, about 38 percent on the *tone* in which it is delivered, and a huge 55 percent on the body language of the speaker. In other words, 93 percent of a good presentation is something other than the words the speaker chooses. Chapter 10 takes a close look at body language. But it's worth pointing out here that you don't want to undo all the work that goes into making your first three minutes work by inadvertently sending the wrong message with your posture or gestures.

Make sure your posture is not at odds with your message. Slouching, putting your hands in your pockets, or rolling your

> **Secrets of the Pros**
>
> "Ninety-three percent of the believability of your message is not the content or words you use. It's not what you say but how you say it."
>
> —Judy Chaffee

eyes all send the message, "I don't *really* want to be here," even if your words say something else.

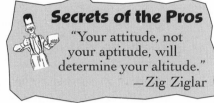

1. *Stand up straight.* A confident posture, with weight distributed evenly on both feet, signals confidence and stability.

2. *Look participants in the eye.* Maintaining eye contact is the number one way to build good rapport. If you can't look individuals in the eye, they will feel you're hiding something from them, no matter what you say. Start with a few friendly faces and then branch out to the rest of the audience.

3. *Be relaxed.* Tension is communicated to an audience as quickly as words. If you're tense and uncomfortable, your audience will respond in kind. (For pointers on relaxation, see chapter 3.)

4. *Use appropriate gestures.* And use a lot of them. Be an animated, dynamic speaker. Vary the force and nature of your gestures. Your audience will appreciate this, especially in the first few moments of a presentation when they are unsure about you.

5. *Be decisive.* Don't "hem-and-haw," especially in the opening beats of your presentation. Make your point, then move on.

6. *Smile.* A smile signals confidence, openness, and relaxation.

Have you ever been at a talk or presentation that just wasn't going well for the speaker? He or she has talked for several minutes. You and the people around you have started squirming a little in your seats. You glance at each other. More than likely the question on everyone's mind is: "Where is this going?"

Avoid this in your own presentations by providing the audience with the big picture. This means spending a little bit of your time telling them what the presentation is all about. In the first chapter we discussed the value of establishing objectives. Spend about thirty seconds of your first three minutes sharing those objectives with your audience.

The First Three Minutes

Practice delivering a relaxed smile in front of a mirror. A smile goes a long way and helps to win an audience over.

7. *Use the first row.* Usually the people who are most open to a speaker take the first row. Draw strength from these audience members. I often say, "Now you folks in the front row are gonna laugh at my jokes, I hope." I also maintain early eye contact with them to draw power from their interest and attention.

8. *Create a conversational tone.* People love having a conversation, but do not like being lectured to. Avoid the tone of a lecture. Ask questions, seek audience opinion, and use plain language and short declarative sentences. (See chapter 6 for more on "Setting the Tone" and having a conversation with your audience.)

> **Secrets of the Pros**
>
> "Even if you keep on giving the same speech over and over again (remember that technique helped make Ronald Reagan president of the United States), always find out the names of some people in the audience and what they especially came for. When you get to that point in your presentation, look across the room and say 'Tom you'll be especially interested in this point.'"
>
> —Dr. Jeffrey Lant

9. *Move among your audience.* If the size of the group allows, walk into the audience as you speak. Avoid podiums whenever possible.

Know How to Gesture Effectively

Gestures are important, especially in your first three minutes. They create a dynamic atmosphere, hold the audience's attention, and communicate what kind of speaker you are. Yet despite their importance, many speakers, even very accomplished ones, take gestures for granted. It's worth the time to study and practice the how-tos of effective gesturing.

Gestures can be grouped into three major categories:

➤ *Descriptive gestures* are used to clarify or enhance a verbal message. They help the audience to understand comparisons and contrasts and to visualize the size, shape, movement, location, function, and number of objects.

➤ *Suggestive gestures* are symbols of ideas and emotions. They help a speaker to create a desired mood or express a particular thought.

➤ *Prompting gestures* are used to help evoke a desired response from the audience.

Gestures are reflective of each speaker's individual personality. What's right for one speaker might not work for you. If you suspect you don't have a dynamic enough presence, there are four simple concepts to be aware of when it comes to gestures and gesturing.

1. Respond naturally
2. Suit the gesture to the words
3. Make your gestures convincing
4. Make your gestures smooth and well-timed

Here is a list of common gestures and how audiences tend to perceive them:

➤ **Pointing:** A common gesture, but one to use sparingly. Pointing your index finger can emphasize a statement, or call attention to an idea, but it can also be taken as an accusation.

➤ **Palms down**: Both palms down indicate weight or decisiveness. A sweeping gesture with one arm, palm down, dismisses something, as in, "We won't even talk about that."

➤ **Palms up:** Both arms, palm up invites a group to stand. It also is a gesture used to ask for something. It can also be taken as an offer, when you're giving out something like an idea worth thinking about.

➤ **Chopping:** A chopping motion with one hand shows where something ends and something else begins. It can also be used to make a point. It's stronger than no gesture, but not as strong as pointing.

➤ **Palm out:** Like a halt signal used by a traffic cop, this gesture slows an audience down. It can be used to move from laughter to seriousness or to introduce a new idea.

➤ **Raised fist:** Shows determination or anger—be careful with this one. It is also, of course, a signal for fighting.

STEP 3. Know the Four Audience Tensions and Work to Alleviate Them

It's not a widely known fact, but every audience, however large or small, has four natural and usually subconscious tensions. Become one of the presenters who is aware of these tensions and begin dealing with them IMMEDIATELY.

The four tensions are between:

1. **The audience and the audience.** Members of the audience don't often know each other well, causing tension and apprehension among audience members.

2. **The audience and the presenter.** For the same reason, audience members feel some natural tension toward the presenter and the presenter has similar feelings toward the audience.

3. **The audience and their materials.** Audience members are often given notepads, pens, pencils, notebooks, and other materials.

4. **The audience and the environment.** An unfamiliar environment is sure to cause tension. Even when they know the room, the speaker and the equipment used will produce tension between the audience and the environment.

Just being aware that these four tensions exist will make you a better presenter. Far too few presenters ever give them any thought. It's a shame, since alleviating these tensions are really a matter of following a few simple, common-sense steps.

> **Secrets of the Pros**
>
> "Always start your speech off by thanking particular people from the host organization. Be just as effusive about them as you can be. Remember, not least, they're writing your testimonials!"
> —Dr. Jeffrey Lant

Audience and Audience

➤ Get the audience up and moving.

➤ Get the audience to shake hands and socialize with one another.

Audience and Instructor

➤ Build audience rapport.

➤ Establish and maintain eye contact.

➤ Smile.

Audience and Materials

➤ Involve the audience with their materials immediately. Don't just leave handouts and notebooks in front of them unexplained.

➤ Instruct the audience to IMMEDIATELY write their names on their materials. This will begin the "ownership process" and reduce tension.

➤ Hand out materials only when participants need it and not before. This reduces tension and keeps the audience from being distracted by their material.

Audience and Environment

➤ Be aware of the environment.

➤ Try to make it as comfortable as possible.

➤ Seek and act upon feedback on comfort issues such as seating, room temperature, lighting, sound volume, etc.

➤ If some comfort issue is beyond your control (hard chairs, poor ventilation) then add breaks to your agenda. Better to have a few extra breaks than to have an uncomfortable audience squirming in their seats.

> **Secrets of the Pros**
>
> "Consider a one-page handout for short presentations."
> —Dale Ware

Very Important Points to Remember

✔ You have about three minutes to win an audience. Make the most of them!

✔ Build rapport by hooking your audience, proving you value their time, and letting them know where you're headed.

✔ Research shows that 7 percent of a presentation's outcome is contingent upon words, 38 percent on tonality and 55 percent on body language. Here are a few tips to maximize the 93 percent that isn't words. It isn't what you say but how you say it!

✔ Know the tensions that every audience member feels and work to ease those tensions during your opening.

Fill in Your Favorite Tips from the Chapter

✔ _____

_____

✔ _____

_____

✔ _____

_____

✔ _____

_____

The First Three Minutes

This chapter reveals:

➤ What credibility means

➤ Tips for proving to your audience that you have the right to be at the front of the room

➤ How to build credibility with any audience in minutes

5

Being Credible

JEARY THEORY

Credibility flows from you to the audience—you must
tell the truth and be real to acquire true credibility.

"To win, we must be believed. To be believed, we
must be believable. To be believable, we must tell the
truth. . . ."

—Gerry Spence

The Scene...

You know your subject and you're well prepared for your first big
presentation out of school, but you've got one problem: your résumé.
How can you let your audience know how much you know when
you've only recently graduated from college? Many of your colleagues (and even some of your audience members) have impressive
credentials; how can you convince them that you know what you're
talking about?

The Solution...

Audiences tend to respond much more to a speaker's presence than
to résumé credentials. As a speaker, always keep in mind that the

audience's impression of you is the single most important factor toward establishing your credibility. That's why it is so important to build rapport and show respect for your audience in the first three minutes of your presentation. A positive rapport lays the foundation for your audience and establishes your honesty. Many experts fail as presenters because they rub the audience the wrong way. Understand the power of establishing your credibility!

Secrets

1. KNOW WHAT REAL CREDIBILITY IS

➤ Know how you will be judged.

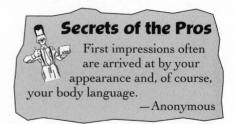

Secrets of the Pros

First impressions often are arrived at by your appearance and, of course, your body language.

—Anonymous

- Depth of knowledge

- Personal experiences

- Level of preparedness

- Enthusiasm during the presentation

- Appearance

- Language (body and verbal)

➤ Is credibility an illusion or reality?

2. TELL THE TRUTH

➤ Commit and adhere to a time-requirement up-front.

➤ Make a note when you say you will do something, then do it!

3. TELL WHY YOU HAVE THE RIGHT TO TALK TO THEM

➤ The more relevant the introduction, the higher your credibility.

➤ Share personal experiences with your audience.

4. CONNECT WITH THE AUDIENCE

➤ Be natural

➤ Be sincere

➤ Be enthusiastic

➤ Be spontaneous

What Is Credibility?

Ever wonder why banks look the way they do? Not necessarily the local branch at the corner, but the big international banks, the Federal Reserve in Washington, D.C., or the huge investment houses on Wall Street. Walking into these banks is a breathtaking experience. Soaring ceilings, vaulted arches, marble floors. In fact only two other types of architectural structures come close to the inspiring drama of a large bank: castles and cathedrals.

Why? Because in all these cases, credibility is paramount. These buildings are large, awe-inspiring, eternal-looking structures that *inspire* credibility. This brings us to the essential paradox of credibility. On the one hand it is very real—what could be more real than the rule of kings, the influence of priests, or the power of bankers? On the other hand, credibility is often subjective and always just an illusion. After all, nothing except God is truly permanent or utterly trustworthy.

> ### Secrets of the Pros
> "One of the things I like to do, whenever possible, is to go around the room and have everyone personally introduce themselves to ME. I'll write down their name and seating position. This helps me get to know and remember them. Throughout the workshop I'll always refer to them by name—it makes them feel important and that the training is more personal."
> —Bob Carmack

The bottom line is this: Credibility is something that is *bestowed* upon one person by one or more other people. It might be the result of hard work; but hard work in and of itself does not build credibility (sad but true). Unless people give you *credit* for the work you do, you can never gain credibility. The trick for you as a presenter is to demonstrate the *qualities* that make people want to bestow credibility upon you.

Credible qualities include:

1. Integrity. Be yourself.

2. Expertise.

3. Empathy.

4. Awareness of your own power.

> ### Secrets of the Pros
> "Let the crowd know you've been 'there.'"
> —Steve Richards

73

The next few sections explain these qualities and provide techniques for demonstrating them to your audience.

Integrity/Be Yourself

Are you honest enough for the audience to believe you? Audiences can see through pretension immediately, and it doesn't take them much longer to see through any of the other forms of dishonesty. You can be sure the audience gets a sense of your integrity by:

➤ Telling the truth: your audience will never really trust you if they catch you in a lie.

➤ Being yourself: trying to be someone you're not is almost as bad as telling a lie. It's also a lot more work.

➤ Doing what you say you will: if you say you're starting at 8:30 A.M., then start at 8:30 A.M. If you promise frequent breaks, allow for frequent breaks.

➤ Speak with conviction: Say it like you mean it, and your audience will believe in your words.

➤ Never pretend to know the answer to a question and *never* fake it. It's better to say "I don't know" and try to help the audience find the answer.

People Want You to Be Honest and to Hear What You Have to Say

W. P. "Buz" Barlow, Jr., a prominent Dallas attorney, took time from his busy practice to serve as Special Counsel to Dr. Robert Schuller. While based at the Crystal Cathedral in Southern California, Buz contributed to *The Hour of Power* television program seen weekly all over the world and spoke to audiences in more than fifty cities across the United States. Upon his return home he was asked to take the pulpit of the prestigious, 8,000-member Lovers Lane United Methodist Church to preach all three Sunday morning services. He relates the following story:

> **Secrets of the Pros**
>
> "Never speak after an animal act or a cute kid. They have tricks you just can't use anymore and retain any credibility at all."
>
> —Dr. Jeffrey Lant

"Having had my own radio show, having done a national television commercial with Steve Allen, and having been a trial lawyer for more than twenty-five years, I've grown accustomed to "performing" under just about any circumstances. I nevertheless found the prospect of bearing my soul to the members of my church family under the watchful eye of my dear friend and mentor, Dr. Don Benton, a formidable task.

"I prayed that I would be worthy of the sacred trust given to me and I prepared as never before to find just the right blend of anecdotes, scriptural references and positive thinking. Don had taught the preaching course at Southern Methodist University's Perkins School of Theology and it was his long-held belief that a message should be scripted, practiced from text, and then delivered without the benefit of notes. I knew I'd let him down if I deviated from this time-tested formula and I had no intention of doing that.

"After countless rewrites, my draft finally completed, I was ready for Dr. Benton to give his blessing to the content and to receive any last-minute advice he deemed appropriate. He sent me off with words of encouragement and some wise counsel I'll never forget, because it applied to every speaking situation imaginable. 'Buz,' he began, 'people want to hear what you have to say and you're obviously well prepared, so now just go out and preach it!'

"'Just preach it' means to give of yourself, to share what is within you rather than to recite memorized lines or worse yet, to merely read from note cards. Without passion and conviction communication at any level suffers. We can't expect anyone to listen if we don't act like what we're saying is important and meaningful to them.

"So always remember to prepare, to practice, and to preach it."

Expertise

As renowned speaker Anthony Robbins suggests, "You don't have to know everything to use everything!" In other words, you don't have to be an expert to have expertise.

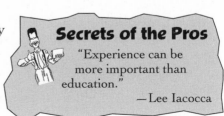

Secrets of the Pros

"Experience can be more important than education."

—Lee Iacocca

Experts are people who have spent their whole life learning about a certain subject. Though I have known many experts who can speak wonderfully, I've also met some real duds. An expert can often get hung up on forcing an audience to see things the way he or she sees it. This alienates an audience and makes the expert, oddly, seem less credible. When an audience doesn't like a speaker, they won't give him credit for the very expertise he spent so much time acquiring.

Secrets of the Pros

"A great way to find out whether you are being authentic or not is to practice in front of teenagers. If you hear, 'You don't sound like yourself, Mom'—even once— you've been given a valuable piece of input."

—Judy Chaffee

It's easier for a good speaker to pick up a basic level of expertise than for a subject matter expert to become a great speaker. Follow these steps to increase your expertise on any subject:

➤ Know your subject; carefully prepare what you will and won't say.

➤ If you're dealing with an unfamiliar subject, do your homework. Request manuals, workbooks, textbooks, training videos, and any other material that can bring you up to speed.

➤ Use the audience's language; learn and use some of the terms your audience knows. This will demonstrate that you took time to prepare.

Enthusiasm

If you are glad to be in front of the room, most audiences will be glad to have you there. Enthusiasm sends the signal that you, the speaker, are comfortable and in control of the situation. The audience will believe in you if you have the confidence and energy to be enthusiastic about your own presentation.

➤ Appeal to emotion; people are persuaded more so by emotion than by logic. The expert sometimes makes the mistake of thinking only logic matters. Combine logic with *emotional* persuasion.

➤ Work the *entire* room; don't fall into the trap of speaking to just one or two people. Speak to everyone in the room. Make eye contact with as many participants as possible. Don't pick favorites!

Empathy

Let your audience know that you understand how things look from their perspective. Prove it by letting them know that you are there for them and not for yourself.

➤ People like people who seem familiar. Identify with your audience and prove that you are one of them. This doesn't mean that you should mimic or patronize them, only that you should strive to see things from their point of view.

➤ Identify with someone the audience admires. Remember back in chapter 1, when you developed a list of people your audience was likely to admire? Let the audience know that you know the people they know. This will help transfer the natural trust they feel for people they admire to you.

➤ Let them know that you understand; listening is hard work. Take breaks, listen to their concerns and seek their feedback.

➤ Dress like your audience dresses; this helps you look and feel like one of them.

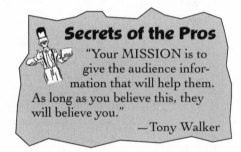

Secrets of the Pros

"Your MISSION is to give the audience information that will help them. As long as you believe this, they will believe you."

—Tony Walker

Awareness of Your Own Power

Believable people know they are believable—and they exude this awareness. You have to convince yourself of your own credibility before you can convince the audience.

➤ Share personal experiences with the audience.

➤ Let them know why you are speaking to them.

Let me share a couple of experiences with you. I went to Zig Ziglar's (my mentor for over fifteen years) home after having seen him present numerous times to thousands of people. I was impressed with how real, credible, and humble Zig is, both in front of a room as well as behind the scenes. You must be real to be credible.

Be the same on stage as off stage. Another good example of this principle is Dr. Ken Blanchard.

I had the opportunity a few years back to meet with him for an hour or so, after a chance encounter in the airport in Dallas. I had listened to him, read his works, and admired him for many years, and to see that he is the same one-on-one as he is in front of groups was a memorable experience for me. I teach people to conduct themselves in front of an audience, in the same manner they would in front of a friend. Be yourself. As Gerry Spence says in his great book *How to Argue and Win Every Time,* people have "imaginary credibility feelers" that sense your realness.

How Your Audience Will Judge You
✓ Depth of knowledge
✓ Personal experiences
✓ Level of preparedness
✓ Enthusiasm
✓ Appearance
✓ Body language

One group of people who understands how important it is to create a perception of credibility in an audience is lawyers. The following are selections from attorney Gerry Spence's terrific book *How to Argue and Win Every Time.*

> "One can stand as the greatest orator the world has known, possess the quickest mind, employ the cleverest psychology, and have mastered all the technical devices of argument, but if one is not credible, one might just as well preach to the pelicans."

> "While the lie detector with its operator may take minutes, even hours to complete its analysis of a single sentence, our minds, as rapidly as the words fall from the speaker's mouth, record split-second conclusions concerning the speaker's credibility."

Tell Them Why You Have the Right to Be in Front of Them

It might be hard for you to believe, but you have the right to be in front of the room. Unfortunately, it is not enough to know this. You must come right out and *tell* the audience

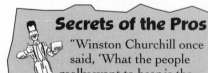

Secrets of the Pros

"Winston Churchill once said, 'What the people really want to hear is the truth. It is an exciting thing to speak the truth.'"

—Gerry Spence

why you have the right to be in front of them. Mention the following when establishing the fact:

1. Your personal experiences
2. Your knowledge and skill as a presenter
3. Your credentials

Your Credentials

Your credentials are important, but they aren't everything. Always be willing to share information on your background and other qualifications with audience members—especially if they ask. However, a long list of your credentials is simply not required. In fact, only a few credentials will really blow an audience away. They are:

➤ President of . . .

➤ Inventor of . . .

➤ Discoverer of . . .

➤ Author of . . .

> ### Secrets of the Pros
>
> "Who is in fact the smartest, most important person in the room? It certainly is not you. After all, the people in the room don't perceive a need for you. You however have a definite need for them. Unless of course you enjoy speaking in a vacuum. Let a crowd believe it is they who are the smartest, most important people in the room and you immediately identify yourself as an inspirational speaker."
> —Steve Richards

Rick Davis spending time one-on-one with Stuart Miller and other participants.

If you're one of these, you're set. Otherwise, you should pick just two or three relevant comments about your experiences that make you a suitable presenter. The key is to make the audience trust you, not

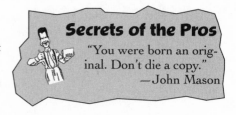

Secrets of the Pros

"You were born an original. Don't die a copy."
—John Mason

knock them out with an amazing list of accomplishments. This, as we have discussed earlier, is determined more by how your audience perceives you as a presenter.

In other words, a long list of credentials doesn't really help that much. If you have a list, keep it brief and to the point. If you don't, don't worry. Your audience will respond more to the fact that you open your talk with great enthusiasm than to the fact that you mention twenty background facts about yourself. Of course, it goes without saying that you should never lie about your credentials. Once you're caught—and you will be—your audience will never believe another word you say.

One More Note: Spontaneity

Fundamental to the success of any presentation is spontaneity, and spontaneity plays an important role in being credible. You can lose a chance to more fully connect with your audience by not taking advantage of an opportunity to be spontaneous. A good joke by an audience member, a piece of timely news, even a mistake you make are all spontaneous moments you can use to win the respect of your audience and thus strengthen your credibility with them.

There's an irony to spontaneity; to be spontaneous, you have to be prepared. Mark Twain once said, "It takes about six weeks to prepare a good ad lib comment." That may sound silly. But the truth is that you can plan spontaneity. Leave space for responding to the unexpected in your agenda. Never be so wed to your plan that you can't detour to go in a promising direction chosen by the audience. To respond with humor and enthusiasm shows great confidence. And to be confident is to deserve credibility!

Join Toastmasters for the purpose of practicing and becoming more comfortable with impromptu speaking.

Very Important Points to Remember

✔ Credibility flows from you to the audience—to be credible, you must inspire the audience to bestow credibility upon you.

✔ It's not enough to possess the qualities of a credible person—you must demonstrate them, both directly and indirectly, as soon as you take the front of the room.

✔ You have the right to be at the front of the room. Make the audience aware that you know this and you will gain their respect.

✔ Your credentials are important but they do not make or break you. When discussing credentials, keep it brief. Your audience cares much more about your attitude toward them than about your résumé!

✔ Always leave room for spontaneity. It makes you look relaxed and natural in front of your audience. These characteristics build credibility.

Fill in Your Favorite Tips from the Chapter

✔ _____

_____

✔ _____

_____

✔ _____

_____

✔ _____

_____

This chapter reveals:

➤ The importance of setting the right tone for your presentation

➤ How tone affects the audience's perception of you

➤ How to establish a conversational tone with even the largest groups

➤ How some little things affect your presentation in a big way

6

Setting the Right Tone

"Nothing great was ever achieved without enthusiasm."
—Ralph Waldo Emerson

The Scene ...

You're delivering a half-day presentation to a group of fifty high-school seniors about business opportunities in your field. The presentation is being held in the high-school library, not an ideal place, because you don't want students to feel bored or overly comfortable due to the familiar surroundings. As the students begin to arrive, their facial expressions suggest that they are regarding this presentation as just another class, despite the flip charts and VCR-monitor set-up you've brought in. What you need is some way to create an atmosphere that wakes these students up— something to set a tone that lets them know *your* presentation is something different.

Secrets of the Pros

"When you're nice to people, they want to be nice back to you."
—Jack Canfield

The Solution . . .

The tone of your presentation—the way it feels to the audience—is the sum of everything you do. From the room you select and the clothes you wear, to the actual words you speak, everything affects the tone of the day. The solution to winning over and inspiring any audience is to set the right tone. You're in charge of the details. The trick is knowing how to organize them to set the appropriate tone. The following is a system that leaves nothing to chance.

Secrets

1. Tone and tonality

➤ Presentation tone refers to more than your tone of voice.

➤ The "feel" of the event creates an atmosphere.

➤ Details are important.

2. Big things

➤ Atmosphere = emotion!

➤ Create a conversation.

➤ Define spectrum—show "Tonometer."

➤ Rate your own presentations!

3. A lot of little things that are really big things

➤ Eye contact

➤ Word choice

➤ Body language

➤ Appearance

➤ Openness

➤ Humor

➤ Enthusiasm

➤ Music

➤ Breaks

➤ Activities

Tone and Tonality

An important part of inspiring your audience is the tone you set. Think of all the different uses there are for the word tone: skin tone, color tones, dial tone, tone of voice, muscle tone—virtually anything can be described in terms of its tone.

When we speak of tone, what we're really describing is the *impression* we get from a presentation. The sum of its obvious and subtle qualities; all the big and little things taken together.

The tone of a presentation IS contingent upon many details that combine to give us the overall impression. Was it enjoyable, inviting, user-friendly? Did participants feel welcome, interested, involved, entertained? Or were they uneasy, confused, and bored? Was the presenter conversational, accessible, confident, inspiring Or disorganized, nervous, and preachy? When we answer questions like these, we're discussing tone. The secret to using *tonality* to inspire an audience is in understanding how tonality works and knowing how to set the tone YOU want.

Many guides to public speaking limit themselves to discussing tone of voice when they discuss tone. Throughout the rest of this chapter, however, we use tone to refer to the way your event feels to audience members. Always remember: *the tone of any event is the sum of all its details, large and small, that the audience perceives.*

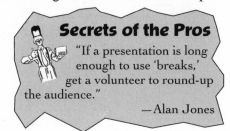

Secrets of the Pros

"If a presentation is long enough to use 'breaks,' get a volunteer to round-up the audience."

—Alan Jones

BIG THINGS

The Atmosphere of Your Presentation

Just as the atmosphere of a restaurant affects the way we perceive our dinner, so the atmosphere of a presentation affects the way we perceive the message. In both cases, consistency is the key to success. If a restaurant has an open, fun, inviting tone, then a quiet reserved waiter can be a let-down. If, however, you're paying big bucks for a formal meal and you get a brash, talkative waiter who likes to hang around and chat, the whole "feel" of your evening can be ruined.

In your presentations, attempt to create an atmosphere that complements your message. Decide on the atmosphere you would like to hear your own message in. Consult your audience research notes (chapter 1) and ask people familiar with your audience what atmosphere your audience is likely to enjoy. Since atmosphere is often an emotional response to surroundings, rather than a logical one, know the emotions most audiences wish to feel. As a rule, most audience members prefer the type of emotion on the left side of the following chart, including "professional audiences" whom we tend to consider reserved or conservative.

Enjoyable atmosphere	Less enjoyable atmosphere
Exciting	Serious
Entertaining	Reserved
Engaging	Solitary
Relaxed	Formal
Lively	Slow
Direct	Wordy
Fun	Showy
Inviting	Closed-off
Loud	Quiet

I've listed some qualities of presenters, both good and bad. The ones on the left will almost always engage an audience and win them over.

Qualities Audiences Love	Qualities Audiences Hate
Conversational	Lecture-oriented (see below)
Open	Reserved
Accessible	Aloof
Knowledgeable	A show-off
Confident	A braggart
Entertaining	Dull
Funny	Rude or insulting
Excited to be there	Perfunctory— I've done this all before
Humility	Arrogance

Get the audience on your side by setting the right tone. Your tone can subtly say what you cannot: "I'm not perfect, so please support me." Then if something goes wrong, you'll have an audience that's willing to help you out. Coach John Wooden says, "Ask the audience for some help in regard to something you appear to have forgotten." They will if you set the right tone.

First impressions are lasting impressions. Your audience will begin responding to you as soon as you start shaking their hands. Likewise, the surroundings you provide have an immediate impact on the atmosphere your audience perceives. Make sure the room sets the tone you want your audience to perceive when they arrive. The following is a checklist of details that will affect the immediate first impression your audience will have:

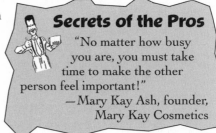

Secrets of the Pros

"No matter how busy you are, you must take time to make the other person feel important!"
—Mary Kay Ash, founder, Mary Kay Cosmetics

❑ Meeting and greeting them—are you open and inviting, or are you aloof and removed?

❑ Type of room—a hotel conference room is different than a high school gymnasium.

❑ Lighting—full bright lights create a high-energy atmosphere.

❑ Room organization—are there boxes lying around and chairs stacked in corners, or is the room orderly and ready-to-go?

❑ Seating arrangement—does the seating encourage interaction or solitude?

For some of the larger business presentations I've helped to design, the client wished to create an atmosphere of high excitement and high energy that participants could sense immediately. The solution? High-energy music as participants arrived and colorful, sporty banners placed throughout the room. In some cases, the presentations were delivered outdoors in large tents, to increase fun and excitement. In this way, participants could sense the carnival-like atmosphere even as they drove up. You might not have the budget for something this outrageous, but a few small things (banners and a tape deck) can have a big impact on the atmosphere of your presentation.

Create a Conversation

Always try to tailor the tone of your presentation to your specific audience. A presentation about charity fund-raising to a local high-school group will require a different tone than a marketing presentation to a group of local bank CEOs (though you might be surprised—bank CEOs are people too, and like to be entertained). The former will require a high "fun factor" (see chapter 8) and an informal atmosphere. The latter will, of course, require a more businesslike atmosphere, but not necessarily at the expense of fun—what I call Business Entertainment—in order to create a memorable event.

When it's all said and done, it basically comes down to a single golden rule:

> **Always attempt to create a conversational tone regardless of audience size.**

Why do people dread attending presentations almost as much as they dread giving them? Because presentations have a reputation for being boring. Why do presentations have a reputation for being boring? Because presenters tend to lecture. No one wants to attend a lecture, yet most everyone enjoys a conversation. You can create a conversational tone with even the largest groups. The key is to set an inviting tone immediately—within the first three minutes.

Having a conversation with even the largest groups

➤ Try to talk *with*, not *at*, your audience.

➤ Use everyday conversational language; avoid big words.

➤ Ask questions *immediately* and listen to the answers.

➤ Get the audience involved, even if it means having them stand and shake each other's hands.

➤ Place nothing between you and your audience—avoid lecterns, podiums, and risers when possible.

➤ Mingle with your audience; when possible, actually walk *into* the audience.

➤ Use participants' names whenever possible and encourage them to use yours.

➤ Smile — it's a natural conversation starter!

➤ Use humor.

➤ Tell stories.

Talk with, not at, your audience, and SMILE A LOT! Plan to use appropriate humor. When professional facilitator David Freeborn talks with the audience about logistics (housekeeping info), he positions it like this: "Well, folks, I've got good news and bad news. The good news is, if you are a smoker you can smoke today! The bad news is, you can't smoke in here!"

The rest of chapter 6 deals with details big and small that affect the tone of your presentations. But if you only adopt one piece of advice from this chapter, make it this: *create a conversation!*

Use the "Tonometer"

The tone of a presentation can be measured on a continuum between a starched and boring LECTURE and a fun and exciting CONVERSATION. The "Tonometer" is a gauge that helps presenters identify what level his or her presentation rates, while in development or even on the day of the presentation. Copy the page and keep it for yourself. You decide which side of the tonometer you want your presentation to be on.

FULL LECTURE   MIX   CONVERSATIONAL/FUN

Tonometer

A LOT OF LITTLE DETAILS THAT ARE REALLY BIG DETAILS

Eye Contact

Eye contact is the cement that binds a speaker and an audience. When you speak, it is your eyes that involve your listeners in your presentation, making it direct, personal, and conversational.

Setting the Right Tone

Conversely, there is no more certain way to break the communication bond than by failing to look at your audience.

No matter how large an audience may be, each listener wants to feel important, to sense a personal connection with the speaker, and to feel that the speaker is communicating directly with him or her. Just as a member of a small, informal group feels excluded from a conversation if the speaker doesn't meet his

> **Secrets of the Pros**
>
> "The real secret of success is enthusiasm. Yes, more than enthusiasm I would say excitement. I like to see men get excited. When they get excited, they make a success of their lives."
>
> —Walter Chrysler

or her eyes, the people in your audience will feel left out if you fail to establish direct eye contact with them.

Your Words

The tone you set has a lot to do with the words you choose and the way you speak them. That's because your diction (the words you choose) and syntax (the way you put those words together) can reveal a lot about your attitude toward your audience. Remember that tone *equals* emotion. What your audience feels is your attitude might as well really *be* your attitude toward them.

The general rule on word choice is to stick close to your everyday diction. This relaxes audience members and creates that all-important conversational tone. Avoid large words—audience members may not know their meaning and they may feel you're trying to show off. Your job is not to impress the audience with your vocabulary, but rather, to communicate your message in the most entertaining, inspiring way.

Another good rule to remember is to avoid words that leave no room for dissent. These types of words beg challenges and may paint you into a corner. For example:

AVOID	USE
Always	Often, usually
Never	Seldom
Certainly	Likely
At no time	Rarely
Forever	Once in a while
Positively	Most likely

Also avoid what I call "IST" language—language that can be taken as sexist, racist, and so on. This has less to do with political correctness than it does with the potential alienation of your audience members. Our goal is to inspire *everyone* in the room to action—100 percent buy-in. An offended or alienated audience member is NOT an inspired audience member.

➤ Avoid stereotypes.

➤ Don't describe people by their looks, age, race, ethnicity, or clothing.

➤ Don't say "girl" when you mean "woman."

➤ Try to use examples that equally employ both genders.

➤ Avoid tired old expressions that carry a negative connotation: "cigarette girl," "old-wive's tale."

➤ Don't assume certain jobs go with a certain gender: businessman, salesman, etc.

Of course, you should never, use profanity. In my opinion, avoid what you might consider even the most harmless sort of off-color language. Why? Because profanity is just that—profane. It can deeply offend audience members and there is no potential payoff that justifies the risk.

Body Language

Research has demonstrated that over half of all human communication takes place on the nonverbal level. The codes that govern nonverbal communication tend to affect us subconsciously, but are nevertheless highly efficient carriers of meaning. Each of us becomes very proficient at sending and interpreting nonverbal signals at a relatively early age. Your posture, gestures, body movements, and facial expressions—all are critical nonverbal elements of your speech delivery system.

Observe the following checklist:

❑ Gestures—Do you use your hands and your head comfortably? Are your gestures compatible with what you are saying?

❑ Facial Expressions—Is your face animated? Does it communicate an interest in your audience and your subject?

❑ Posture—Do you stand alert and erect, without being stiff? Going back on one hip, placing your hands in your pocket, pacing back and forth—all suggest that you'd rather be somewhere else.

❑ Body Movement—Do your movements and changes in body positions serve a communicative purpose? Do they focus attention on the subject at hand?

Your Dress and Appearance

Naturally you'll want to take time to groom well for any presentation appearance. Unless you're Albert Einstein, uncombed hair and disheveled clothing will make an audience perceive that you didn't care enough to clean up for them.

How you dress also counts. Whenever possible, dress like your audience. This will set them at ease and set an "I'm-one-of-you" tone. We live in the age of business casual—so if your audience will be in polo shirts and khaki pants, they'll feel more comfortable if you are too. If you don't know *what* your audience will be wearing, the general rule is to dress up a little. You can always remove a suit jacket to become less formal, but it's hard to turn jeans and a sweatshirt into business wear.

➤ Press your clothes whenever possible—even casual clothes. This gives an impression of crispness and neatness.

➤ If you're wearing a suit, keep the jacket buttoned until you're ready to make a "let's roll our sleeves up and get to it" impression.

➤ Different colors mean different things. Loud colors can seem confident but can also seem aggressive. Darker colors can appear subdued but also dull. Know what works for you.

Your Openness

Part of any winning tone has to do with your openness as a presenter. You can say you're open to your audience — that you're accessible, caring and conscientious. But actions speak louder than words. Demonstrate that you are open to your audience by taking the following steps:

➤ Ask questions regularly; then LISTEN to how your audience responds. Chapter 11 deals with question-and-answer techniques, but here are a few pointers:

- Listen to the entire question.
- Make sure you understand that the question you're hearing is the one that is being asked.
- Repeat the question so everyone can hear it.
- Don't make up an answer if you don't know the answer.
- NEVER put-down or poke fun at an audience member's question.

➤ Sincerely seek audience feedback, then act on it. If you ask your audience whether they're too cold and they say yes, you better turn the heat up.

➤ On breaks, talk to your audience members on an individual basis. This lets them know you're down-to-earth and accessible.

➤ Acknowledge positive behavior and explain how it affects others.

➤ Ask for participants' ideas and flip chart them when possible.

➤ All ideas are good ideas — give compliments freely.

➤ Ask for comments or examples from participants.

➤ Talk about your own experiences.

➤ Don't hesitate to admit you may be wrong.

➤ Give complete instructions.

Appeal to Emotion

We cannot underestimate the importance of emotion in the presentation equation. We have all made decisions based on emotional reasons. As J. P Morgan once said, "A person usually has two reasons for doing something. One that sounds good and the real reason."

93

That real reason is almost always based upon emotion. In other words, we think with our logical faculties, and act on our emotional biases.

Remember:

➤ People take action based on emotion.

➤ Believe in what you say—say what you believe.

➤ Be aware of audience expression, body language, and feedback. It is a gauge of their receptivity.

➤ Talk with your eyes; speak from your heart.

Humor

Humor is an international language. Everyone enjoys a laugh. But humor is more than joke telling. Funny and dynamic humor definitely generates positive energy, but that doesn't mean you should try to be a comedian. Your goal is to present a message,and humor is another way to enhance your effectiveness.

There are two guidelines for using humor in presentations. First, share the laughter generated by the audience and second, laugh at personal mistakes. You can never go wrong by making yourself the butt of a joke. The ability to laugh at oneself shows confidence and generosity—two things that go a long way in the presentation business. Here are some basic directions to follow when creating and using humor.

➤ Use yourself as the butt of a joke—avoid humor that makes you look powerful and smart. That looks like bragging and turns people off.

➤ Draw stories from real life rather than using canned jokes.

➤ If you insist on using a joke, borrow one you've seen work before groups and make sure it doesn't contain any of the potentially dangerous elements previously discussed.

➤ Don't short-circuit a joke by overpromising—never say, "I'm gonna tell you a great joke."

➤ Likewise, don't apologize for not being a comedian. Never preface humor with, "I'm not very funny, but here goes." It destroys the fun for everyone.

➤ Keep it short and sweet. Clever wording is usually short and precise wording. Make your humor work the same way.

➤ Speak clearly. A clever comment doesn't work if it has to be repeated.

Enthusiasm

Speak with enthusiasm and conviction and sincerity will follow. Studies prove that those three traits—enthusiasm, conviction, and sincerity—top the list of characteristics audiences most appreciate in a speaker. Enthusiasm is contagious, so be enthusiastic with your delivery. Psychologists tell us that people don't act, they only react. Your enthusiasm will get attention and increase audience interest levels.

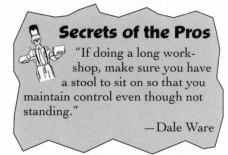

Secrets of the Pros

"If doing a long workshop, make sure you have a stool to sit on so that you maintain control even though not standing."

—Dale Ware

Jokes

A young man is sentenced to twenty years in prison and on his first day in the cell he hears someone down the cellblock shout out, "22!" Everyone within earshot, including his new cellmate, cracks up with laughter. A few minutes later, someone else shouts out, "86!" Again, laughter everywhere.

"What's that all about?" the young man asks his new cellmate when the commotion has ended.

"Well, everyone's been in here so long that we've numbered our jokes," replies the old-timer. "That way instead of telling the whole thing, we can just shout the number when we want a laugh."

Being a congenial young man and eager to make friends, the young prisoner decides he'll give everyone a laugh and the next opportunity he has he shouts, "22!" Not a soul laughs. So he tries again, shouting," 86!" Dead silence. Wounded, he turns to his cellmate and asks what went wrong.

The older, wiser man pauses for a moment, then shakes his head. "Some people," he says, just don't know how to tell a joke."

Aristotle, the father of rhetoric, taught that the great speaker is a good man—his convictions won't permit him to appeal to unworthy motives. So you're keeping good company when you speak with high enthusiasm. Audiences are quick to detect an unworthy attitude. They respond to the constructive and the positive. That's why speaking with wholesome conviction is admired so universally.

> Let's face it: HUMOR IS RISKY. The bigger the risk the bigger potential for a laugh AND the bigger potential for offending someone. Remember they may or may not remember the joke or the laugh, but they will definitely remember if they were offended. Once you have personally offended someone, you have lost them. The trick is to maximize the laugh potential and minimize the offend potential.
>
> —Dan Finocchiaro
> Professional Trainer and
> Stand-up Comic

Some smaller details that are important

Here are a handful of ideas that can make audience members even more comfortable and set an enjoyable, conversational tone. Many of them are mentioned elsewhere in this book. But be aware that they exist and use them for your benefit!

Music: Play some! Music is the universal mood setter. As a background it can underlie everything we do and say. Use music to make your presentations more exciting. High-energy, upbeat music helps set the right tone for any presentation.

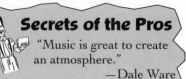

Secrets of the Pros

"Music is great to create an atmosphere."
—Dale Ware

Breaks: Take them—frequently! Sitting still is hard work for adults. Let attendees know you understand this by providing frequent breaks—at least one every sixty to ninety minutes. Also, a listener who desperately needs to use the restroom or stretch her legs is definitely not paying 100 percent attention to what you have to say. Always set a specific TIME to return and start back up. (See chapter 10 for more on breaks.)

Activities: Use some. Activities get the audience up and moving. Even the most somber group of business people respond to fun, appropriate activities that make a point. People remember 10 percent of

---

Enthusiasm

You can do anything if you have enthusiasm.
Enthusiasm is the yeast that makes your hopes rise to the stars.
Enthusiasm is the sparkle in your eye. It is the swing in your gait,
 the irresistible surge of your will and your energy to execute your ideas.
Enthusiasts are fighters.
They have fortitude.
They have staying quality.
Enthusiasm is at the bottom of all progress.
With it there is accomplishment.
Without it there are only abilities.

—Henry Ford

---

what they read, 20 percent of what they hear, 30 percent of what
they hear and see—and up to 80 percent of what they see, hear,
and do. Get them involved by using "Business Entertainment."
See chapter 8 for more details.

Very Important Points to Remember

✔ The tone you establish determines how the audience perceives
you; if they approve, you will get 100 percent buy-in.

✔ Everything counts when you're establishing tone. Know how to
create the right atmosphere.

✔ Create a conversational tone—no matter what the occasion!

✔ People respond to emotion. Make sure everything you say and
do works both intellectually and emotionally.

Fill in Your Favorite Tips from the Chapter

✔ _____
_____

✔ _____
_____

✔ _____
_____

This chapter reveals:

➤ The importance of doing even more than is expected in your presentations

➤ How to set and exceed expectations

➤ How to use your audience members' names

➤ How to make audience members the stars of your presentation

7

Exceeding Expectations

JEARY THEORY

In order to exceed expectations you must understand your audience—know what they want. Then deliver more!

"When we do more than we are paid to do, eventually we will be paid more for what we do."

— Zig Ziglar, speaker and author

The Scene ...

You're not exactly a beginner at presentations—you know how to get an audience excited and you know how to deliver what they expect. But now you're at the stage where you want to do something more. You've seen other presenters who always seem to have a little something extra that just blows the audience away. But there's so much to remember just getting your presentation up and

Secrets of the Pros

"An audience expects you to do a good job— that's customer satisfaction. It's those 'little extras' you do that can make your presentation memorable and create 'customer delight.'"

— David Freeborn

99

running, how are you ever going to remember those little extras that please audiences so much?

The Solution . . .

Up to this point we've discussed what your presentation must have to make it successful. If you simply follow the steps and bulleted points outlined in the previous chapters you'll be well on your way to having successful presentations. But you can virtually assure yourself of the 100 percent audience buy-in that leads to true inspiration by going a few steps further. Often audiences respond as well when they receive small things they didn't expect as when they get the large things that they came for. Become known as a presenter who delivers that little something extra. The following secrets will show you how.

Secrets

1. **Give value—do more than is expected.**

2. **Know your audience's wants, needs, and desires.**

3. **Establish expectations early in the presentation.**

   ➤ Define what the presentation is and isn't.

   ➤ Define what it can and can't do.

   ➤ Define your role (facilitator, expert, entertainer, trainer, etc.).

4. **Under-promise, over-deliver.**

5. **Learn and use names.**

   ➤ Using name badges correctly makes a big difference.

   ➤ Know what to do with nicknames.

   ➤ Memorize a few names to get started.

6. **Create winning opportunities for your audience.**

7. **Always hold a little back in reserve.**

   ➤ Keep deliverables in reserve—have several aces in the hole to surprise the audience.

8. **Prepare those little extras—examples of what you have to offer.**

Give Value—Do More than Is Expected

This has been my motto for years. The one thing everyone has in common is that they love getting a little bit more than they paid for. It can be almost anything—an extra few hours of commitment, a card that sums up the points of a presentation, even pictures of an event or presentation. If they didn't expect it, it blows them away when you prepare it. In fact, I'm personally willing to say this: 90 percent of all the effort I put into a job is making sure I satisfy what a client wants. If I stop there, I can almost always make my client happy by giving them what they paid for. But if I add an extra 10 percent, I can have a completely thrilled client. Why? Because they got more than they had coming. Guess what they remember most: the 90 percent of the effort that went into making sure I gave them what they asked for, or the 10 percent that went into the little extras that blew them away?

The same is true for your presentations. When someone hires you (or invites you or accepts your offer to volunteer) as a presenter, they expect you to accomplish the goal of communicating a message to an audience. Once they arrive, your audience expects this as well. The bad news is this: everyone pretty much takes for granted all the effort you put into making a presentation work. Audiences expect the room to be in order, the tone to be inviting and the speaker to be prepared and entertaining.

There is good news, though: however demanding (or easy-to-please) an audience may be, as long as you accomplish the task of delivering the presentation reasonably well, they will be reasonably pleased. Here's the great news: Once you've covered those basics, you can blow your audience away by adding a few simple little extras that will make them remember your presentation for years to come. Literally. The way to do this is to make sure you really know what they want, then figure out a way to give a little more while they aren't looking.

Know Your Audience's Deepest Needs and Desires

If you have analyzed your audience, you'll have a clear idea of what they want. Your presentation should be geared from the start to please the particular audience you are speaking to, be they car salespeople, ministers, or lawyers. But audiences are people, too.

101

This means they have a whole host of needs, desires, and wants that go far beyond the topic you're there to talk about. In addition to their obvious conscious desire to be entertained and informed in an open, inviting, and comfortable atmosphere (see chapters 2 through 6) audiences also have at least seven subtle and unconscious desires. Everyone wishes to:

1. Belong
2. Be respected
3. Be appreciated and liked
4. Be safe
5. Be successful
6. Find romance
7. Be enthused

This is not to say that you can (or should even try to) meet and exceed all seven of these subconscious desires. It is to say that you should be well aware of them. When you deliver the extras that please audiences you'll be aiming much more toward these subconscious and emotional desires than at the conscious and rational ones I mentioned above.

Little Things Sell Big Things

Fact: If you want someone to buy something big, toss in something small for free. A friend of mine, John Bacon, calls it the "Cracker Jack"™ syndrome. Not everybody buys a box of Cracker Jack™ for the caramel corn and peanuts, however delicious you might think they are. Why do some buy it? For that little 2¢ prize at the bottom.

Another friend remembers buying his first new car, which represented a huge investment for him. While showing it off to his next-door neighbor, he opened the glove box, and found a pair of brown cotton gloves with an attached note scrawled on the back of the salesman's business card. "These are in case you ever have to change a tire," he had written. My friend remembers the $1.50 pair of gloves, though he now has a hard time remembering the price of that car.

As I pointed out in chapter 6, human beings think with their rational minds, but act upon (and remember) emotions. If you deliver little extras, your audience will be much more likely to buy-in to the big things you came to deliver.

Establish Expectations Early in the Presentation

One mistake you can make is failing to agree upon a reasonable level of expectations very early in the presentation. Although it doesn't have to be within the first three minutes of your presentation (see chapter 4), you shouldn't wait much longer to ask your audience what their expectations are. The following three-step process almost always works for me:

1. I outline *my* expectations for the day. I do this by revealing my objectives, the topic and main ideas I will cover, as well as the agenda.

2. I make three commitments up front: I commit to delivering 1) valuable, usable information; 2) as excellent a presentation as I can; and 3) fun. For these three commitments I ask the audience to make one commitment: to get involved.

3. I ask the audience for *their* expectations. I write these in one- or two-word bullet points on a flip chart, then review them, pointing out which expectations are realistic and which are not.

Not only does this system put the audience in the driver's seat, it also results in a page that "puts everything on the table" and allows us to fine-tune and come to an agreement on what the presentation can and cannot do. If you use this approach, it will serve as a sort of contract between you and the audience and guarantees that you will come a long way toward meeting their expectations—because they're clearly defined for everyone in the room to see.

Early on in any presentation, most presenters feel a strong urge to make big promises that will excite their audience. Not a bad idea— as long as they can deliver the goods. The problem is, we might exaggerate a little. In so doing, we set up our own failure the way a high jumper sets up his own failure if he sets the bar too high. Nowhere is this urge to promise big as strong as when you discuss objectives and expectations with the audience. There's a rule to remember here and that rule is:

Under-Promise, Over-Deliver

Making promises we can't keep is a bad habit that's easy to fall into. Often in our everyday lives we're tempted to promise things we know will be difficult—whether we're promising to spend more time with our families or to deliver something at work or to meet a friend. Sometimes the reason we do this is because promising is easier than facing the truth of the matter—that we might not have time, can't get the job done in time, or don't want to meet the friend. Think of how many times you've been in a jam for promising more than you could deliver!

The temptation to promise more than you can deliver in a presentation is at least as strong as in everyday life. After all, you can really dazzle your audience with an opener that promises to answer all their questions, keep them entertained, and make them rich. However, audiences are very shrewd. They'll start to catch on quickly that you're not backing up your promises—that you're failing to deliver value. Once that happens, you'll have a hard time keeping your credibility level high. Solve this problem by not promising too much. If you keep the level of expectation within reason—by not overpromising—then your audience will be thrilled when they get MORE than they expected!

Avoid Promising Too Much

Overpromising is like charging up a credit card: it feels good for a moment but later you have to pay up—sometimes more than you can afford. Here are a few common situations where the temptation to overpromise will be strong. Don't fall into the trap!

➤ *Don't promise to deliver more value than you can.* "By the time you're done with this presentation you'll know more about this topic than your bosses do." (Try this: "I promise to use all the skill I have to make this information easy to understand and to make this presentation fun!")

➤ *Avoid promises about things you can't control.* Don't promise a great lunch or an early ending time or great future success unless you can guarantee it.

➤ *Avoid promising that things will occur at specific times.* If you promise that lunch will be at noon and it's ten minutes late, you have

failed. If you under-promise by saying we'll get to lunch as
early as possible, depending on how much material we cover,
then no one will know lunch was ten minutes late and you're
still a hero.

➤ *When asked when the presentation is scheduled to end, be conservative
in your estimate.* Even people who want to listen to you like to
know when the talk will end. Create your presentations so that
you have plenty of extra time. If you know your talk will take
till 2:00 P.M., then announce your scheduled closing time as
3:00. That way if you're ten minutes **late** finishing your audience will feel they are getting out fifty minutes early.

➤ *Don't build up jokes or segments of your talk beyond what you can
realistically deliver.* Many a good joke has been killed by too great
a build-up. When you say something like, "Let me tell you the
funniest joke I ever heard in my life," you set the bar very high
indeed. Just tell the joke. An unexpected bit of humor is always
better than an expected one. Likewise, use short transitions
between sections of your talk. Avoid the temptation to "build
up" the next topic you're going to talk about.

Learn and Use Names

Names are extremely powerful tools that far too few presenters
ever take advantage of. Have you ever bought something else then
gone back and had the clerk remember your name? Or better yet,
the names of your children or friends? If you have, odds are you
were mighty impressed. That's the power of names. Names are
powerful because we intrinsically understand that, when someone
uses our name, that person has acknowledged our specialness.
Since most people have trouble remembering and using names,
they don't expect others—even speakers and presenters—to have
that ability. That means names provide a great opportunity for
impressing your audience and delivering that extra touch that
inspires them.

Some speakers have the power to remember everyone's name in a
room without the use of name badges or other props—even in
very large groups. If you're one of these, then congratulations!
Your job has just become a whole lot easier. If you're like the rest
of us, then take heart. Most audience members will have a hard

time remembering your name and won't expect you to remember or use theirs. Following the steps I outline below for getting more mileage out of your audience's names is a great bonus for you and for them.

Memorizing Names

My friend John Bacon has the uncanny knack of remembering the name of every person in a room of even a hundred people. I asked him how he does it, and what follows is what he said.

Learning the names of fifty or even a hundred people in a few minutes might seem like magic, but it isn't. The point is that I go to the trouble of meeting each audience member *individually*, before the presentation. I get their names, one by one, and commit them to memory. Easy! If this sounds ridiculous, consider how many people you know—by name and face—right now. It's likely to be in the thousands (even higher if you include famous names and faces of people you've never met). Adding a few more audience members isn't all that hard, but it takes concentration. If you're interested in picking up the trick of knowing everybody's name, try this:

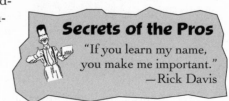

Secrets of the Pros

"If you learn my name, you make me important."
—Rick Davis

1. Meet each audience member as soon as possible. Make eye contact with that person and shake hands. When you ask for his or her name—LISTEN! I mean *really* listen.

2. Repeat the name at least twice. "Good morning, Joe. Nice to meet you. Come on in and have a seat, Joe."

3. As you survey the room before your talk starts, silently remind yourself of each person's name. "That's Joe, that's Mary." Don't be afraid to ask for the name once or twice more. And don't be afraid to ask a few questions of audience members, using their names liberally while you're doing this.

You don't need to take a memory improvement class to make this work. But you have to be committed to learning your audience's names. Most of us can't remember names because we don't take the time to really listen when we're being introduced to someone. Take the time to listen and you'll be shocked at how easily you can master the names and faces of even a large group.

In general, you'll want to use names whenever possible. Use first names when:

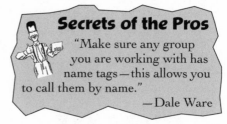

Secrets of the Pros

"Make sure any group you are working with has name tags—this allows you to call them by name."

—Dale Ware

➤ you call on someone with a question.

➤ you are repeating that person's question for the rest of the group to hear.

➤ you are answering a question someone has asked.

➤ you are praising someone or offering a compliment.

➤ you are asking someone to join you at the front of the room.

Whenever possible try to get a list of names in advance so that you can practice pronouncing them. Nothing sends a signal that you don't care faster than mispronouncing a name. If in doubt, ask for the correct pronunciation—then use it!

Know How to Use Name Badges

The next-best thing to remembering every name in the room is to use name badges (depending on the size of your audience). They are powerful tools, but too often people don't use them correctly. Audience members are usually handed a blank sticker upon which they scrawl their own name and then stick it on a jacket or sweater that comes off during the presentation. Remember, when you really NEED the name is when you're at the front of the room presenting and wish to call on someone. If the name badges are written in different handwritings and with different pens, you'll never be able to read them.

A little pre-planning provides easy solutions to the problem.

➤ Whenever possible use pre-prepared name badges. These can be written out by hand from a list of participants ahead of time. Or you can type all the names on a sheet of paper then slide them into clip-on name badge sleeves available at most office-supply stores.

➤ When you prepare name tags, place the first name above (rather than before) the last name, center the first name and put it in larger print than the last name. The first name is the one you'll need when you're at the front of the room.

Right way	**Wrong way**

➤ Keep blank name tags on hand: if you spell someone's name incorrectly they'll say it's okay. IT IS NOT OKAY! Immediately get rid of the misspelled name badge and correct it on a blank name badge. Names are powerful. Never misspell a name!

➤ If you are using hand-printed name tags, print them yourself or have an assistant print them as participants arrive. This makes for a standard printing style and a more legible name tag.

➤ Ask participants to keep their name tags in plain view.

➤ Wear a badge with your name on it. Be one of them!

A Thought on Nicknames

There are two schools of thought on nicknames. Many presenters use them liberally and, I think, presumptuously. Other presenters use them only after they've been invited to use them. You can probably guess which group I'm in. In general, an audience member will let you know if she prefers a nickname to her given name. If so, use it. And if you're using a preprinted name badge with the participant's formal name, write a new one.

If a participant's name badge says William, then he is not Will, Bill, Billy, or any other variation unless he invites you to call him that. If William Shakespeare walked into your presentation, you wouldn't want to be remembered as the person who called him Bill all day long.

Create Winning Opportunities for Your Audience

A good friend of mine has a phrase he likes to remind himself of whenever he makes a presentation: "Let your audience be the

---

How to have a one-on-one conversation with 500 people at the same time

I was presenting to a large convention in New Orleans. There were about five hundred people in the room and I was doing a ninety minute presentation on communications skills. It was early in my career as a speaker and I was dutifully looking over the entire room, making eye contact here and there and making sure no one felt left out.

After the presentation was over, several people thanked me for the attention I had given them during the talk. They all said, "I feel like you were talking to me personally." That's why the talk was so good. It impressed me, because even though I was making eye contact I was not speaking to any one in particular. I learned from that one event the single most important lesson I ever learned about audiences. Make your talk a one-on-one conversation—just do it with several hundred people at the same time.

—Bob Gerold

hero." What this means is that audience members are like everyone else on the planet, they wish to be respected, seen as intelligent, and praised in front of their peers. Use this information to make sure your audience members feel as if they are "winning" when they listen to one of your presentations.

Level One Opportunities

There are two different ways to do this. I call them Level One and Level Two winning opportunities. Level One winning opportunities are those moments that simply occur—an audience member tells a funny joke, asks a good question, or answers a question as well as or better than you could. In these instances, repeat the comment, wisecrack, question or answer so the entire group can hear it and then *praise her for what she did*. Never underestimate the power of praise and encouragement. An impromptu winning opportunity such as this will do a number of things:

➤ It will make the individual you point out feel great.

➤ It will reduce the anxiety audience members have of joining in by making them see that you will recognize their efforts.

➤ It will create a feeling of audience buy-in to the presentation — most audiences are willing to meet you halfway if you pay attention to them.

➤ It will create a feeling of pride and ownership among the audience when they see that you endorse what they say.

Level Two Opportunities

Level Two winning opportunities are opportunities that you create, rather than wait for, in order to make your audience the hero. This includes asking questions that audience members can answer — then letting them answer the questions fully. When an audience member answers one of your questions correctly, all sorts of great things happen. For one thing, the audience member feels good about himself and will want to answer more of your questions. Additionally, other audience members will want to jump on the bandwagon, creating a good dynamic between you and the audience.

Here are a few ways you might create winning opportunities for your audience:

➤ Get audience members involved: assign them bits of information you'll deliver in your presentation then let THEM deliver the information.

➤ Ask for volunteers from the group to help you make a point, when appropriate. Magicians use audience members as helpers to create credibility and audience buy-in — so should you!

➤ Call for applause when an audience member comes to the front of the room. Don't embarrass them with applause when they merely answer a question correctly, but when they assist you in some way (writing on flip charts, delivering a set of bullet points), remember to say something like, "How about a nice hand for James."

➤ Always give credit to the audience: don't make the mistake of telling an audience member's joke as if you made it up. Be sure to repeat a participant's comment so that others can hear it — then give that person his or her credit so the group can see how fair you are and that they will be rewarded for any risks they take.

The object is to make your audience the heroes by bringing attention to them and not to yourself. They'll remember your presentation because they (not you) were the center of attention.

Always Hold a Little Back In Reserve

It's a good idea to always hold back a small surprise for your audience while you're giving a presentation. This can be nearly anything you can imagine—a joke, some giveaways, a piece of information they didn't think they would get, an early departure time, a laminated card with the five top points of your presentation on it. The key element in making these little things work is surprise. A magician's tricks work because he doesn't let the audience know exactly what's going to happen until it happens.

Be like a magician. If you plan to hold something back in order to surprise your audience, you may be tempted in your excitement to let the cat out of the bag. Don't! Hold your trump card back so that you can wow your audience when they least expect it. Just as timing is all-important to what a magician or comedian does, knowing what to hold back is equally important to a presentation. Remember, most of the fun in a surprise isn't what you get so much as the delight that someone went to the trouble of surprising you!

Some of the Extras You Might Prepare:

❑ scented markers

❑ specially prepared handouts

❑ comical overheads

❑ cards laminated with your (or better, the audience's) own words written out

❑ funny handouts, pictures, and recordings

❑ pens, pins

❑ a simple handout summing up what you've covered

The idea is to deliver these extras with a little pizzazz. Don't ruin the surprise by telling the audience what you have in mind. This serves two purposes. One, it gives the audience the pleasure of a surprise. And two, it allows you to be seen as someone who goes beyond mere expectations. A little goes a long way when it comes to exceeding the audience's expectations. The best way to stay on top of the game is by not making things too hard for yourself by promising too much!

One Last Word: Remain Flexible

Most audiences don't expect much flexibility from presenters. Surprise them by being the kind of person who can meet them half way. Changing part of the order of your presentation, adding or removing

something, or taking an un-
scheduled break all signal
flexibility to an audience.
Even moving your presen-
tation to another room or
outdoors can be the little
something extra that makes
an audience remember your
presentation. Don't be afraid
to experiment.

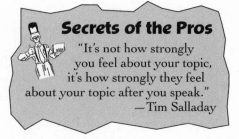

Secrets of the Pros

"It's not how strongly
you feel about your topic,
it's how strongly they feel
about your topic after you speak."
—Tim Salladay

Very Important Points To Remember

✔ Everyone loves something extra; take care to know your audience and their expectations, then exceed those expectations.

✔ Hold a little back so that you can provide "little extras" that
wow your audience.

✔ Create winning opportunities for your audience—make your
audience the hero!

✔ Most audiences expect dry, dull presentations. Exceed expectations by learning your audience's names, by speaking in plain
English and using humor.

Fill in Your Favorite Tips from the Chapter

✔ _____

_____

✔ _____

_____

✔ _____

_____

✔ _____

_____

PART 3
The Body of Your Presentation

This chapter reveals:

➤ The difference between how presenters speak and audiences think and what that means to you

➤ How to create "peaks of interest" throughout your presentation

➤ How to heat up your presentation by gaining and maintaining audience involvement

➤ How to use "Business Entertainment" to keep your audience on the edge of their seat

8

Keeping Their Attention

Because the average adult has an attention span of five to seven minutes, you should manage your presentations in a way that gets your point across and keeps your audience at the highest possible level of interest.

"People will pay more to be entertained than educated."
—Johnny Carson

The Scene...

Your presentation started out with energy and excitement. But now that you've gotten into the nitty-gritty you can sense that your audience's energy level is ebbing. The facts and figures you're presenting are pertinent and your audience should be interested, but they just aren't motivated anymore. How do you get your audience back to the level of excitement they were at during the first three minutes of your presentation?

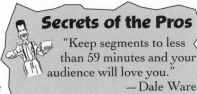

Secrets of the Pros

"Keep segments to less than 59 minutes and your audience will love you."
—Dale Ware

115

The Solution . . .

Give your audience a dose of business entertainment to wake them up—then give them booster shots throughout the day to keep them interested. Understanding how your audience's attention span works is the key to solving the problem. The following are some secrets to ensure that your audiences will be as fresh and interested at the conclusion, as they were the moment your presentation began:

Secrets

1. **Use business entertainment to keep your audience interested.**

    ➤ People think four times faster than they speak.

    ➤ Know your audience's natural highs and lows.

    ➤ Keep your audience excited by including a jolt of business entertainment every five to seven minutes.

2. **Know when and how to use the following business entertainment crowd pleasers:**

    ➤ Music

    ➤ Games

    ➤ Stories

    ➤ Audio-visual aids

    ➤ Breaks—intermission for business entertainment

    ➤ Freebies

The Adult Attention Span

The average adult has an attention span of between five and seven minutes. If you didn't realize that, you can bet the marketers who convinced you to buy the clothes you're wearing or the car you're driving did.

The adult attention span is the reason that commercial breaks in prime-time TV programming last about three to four minutes and why most pop songs rarely go much longer than five or six minutes. Even when we're getting multisensory stimulation (that is, getting information not only by hearing words, but also by seeing, feeling, smelling, or tasting), you can still only count on the average person's attention for five to seven minutes.

If the brevity of the adult attention span is problematic for television producers and song writers, then it's a veritable nightmare for the presenter. Five to seven minutes is barely enough time to walk to the front of the room and inform your audience about the day's subject matter.

Considering the fact that even a short presentation lasts about an hour, overcoming the challenge of your audience's attention span would be challenging enough. But it gets worse . . .

The Relationship Between the Mind and the Mouth

The problem with the relationship between the mind and the mouth is this: the average presenter speaks at about 120 to 200 words per minute. But the average listener can comprehend between 600 and 800 words per minute. This means your audience is thinking at an average of *four times faster than* you can give them information to think about. That gives your audience's collective mind plenty of time to race ahead of you. Couple this with your audience's five- to seven-minute attention span and what you've got—if you're not careful—is a room full of people miles away from you and your presentation.

> **Secrets of the Pros**
>
> "Do use props, demonstrations, activities to let audience 'experience' key points. Don't just use lecture . . . boring, puts people to sleep."
>
> —Dave Terrell

There is a little good news. Your audience will have a high level of natural interest in the first few minutes of your presentation—they'll be feeling you out, trying to decide whether it's worth their time to listen, and probably paying a lot of attention. This means you get a free ride, as far as keeping them interested goes, for the first few minutes. The other natural "attention spike" occurs as soon as you utter the words, "In closing." As soon as the audience realizes the presentation is nearly over, they're awake again, nearly as interested as they were at the opening. The problem is keeping them interested in that vast attention-span desert between the beginning and end. Luckily, there's a solution.

Business Entertainment

Business entertainment is a concept I've been using for some time. I developed it to address the twin problems I've outline above. It stands to reason that if you want to grab an audience's attention and keep it you need to use hooks *throughout your presentation*. It means using attention-grabbers of all different types to involve the audience. Remember, they are thinking way ahead of what you're saying.

Research supports the common sense behind business entertainment. For years psychologists have maintained that the adult attention span is *increased* and learning *enhanced* by:

➤ An uninhibited environment

➤ Creative approaches to solving problems

➤ Allowing mistakes to be made

➤ Constructive and timely feedback

➤ Experiential learning (that is, doing instead of hearing)

And here's another interesting set of statistics on retention. The average adult retains:

➤ 10% of what he reads

➤ 20% of what he hears

➤ 30% of what he sees

➤ 50% of what he hears and sees

➤ 70% of what he says . . . and

➤ 90% of what he says and does

That means if you want your audience to remember, to become inspired by, and to act upon one word you say in ten, then give them a lecture and make them listen. If, on the other hand, you want to get your audience inspired by nine in ten words you say, then get them saying and doing it *themselves*. That's business entertainment!

Another approach to the same problem is practiced by presentation guru David Peoples. He calls his solution "Hot Spice," and his book, *Presentations Plus*, is worth reading for the section on Hot Spice alone and how to employ it in your talks. Peoples compares his idea of Hot Spice to a funnel—by adding a dash of hot spice to your talk every six to eight minutes, you achieve a "funnel" of attention and interest that allows you to get the information into your audience's minds. It's a little different approach, but if it works, try it, and read David Peoples' book!

Using Business Entertainment

Now that you know the WHY behind business entertainment, let's take a minute to cover the HOW. Remember—we're trying to solve two problems at once. First, the human mind has a tendency to wander during a lecture, thereby retaining very little of what is heard. Second, even a very engaging activity will lose its appeal for the average person after a period of time.

That means business entertainment has three goals:

1. To employ some activity, event, point, change, or other eye-opener to break up the monotony of your speaking voice.

2. To select an eye-opener that uses something other than words to jolt the audience and make your point. Ideally it should involve the audience saying and doing.

3. To add a "fun factor."

This will revitalize your audience during the natural lows in their attention span and increase their retention of what you have to say. Below are some of the activities and eye-openers you might consider using.

Games, Skits, Activities, and Other Audience-Involvers

Games, skits, and activities are simply the best types of business entertainment going. Why? Because they get the audience up and moving, saying and doing. And a little friendly competition REALLY wakes up the room.

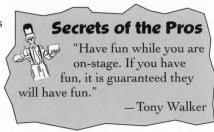

Secrets of the Pros

"Have fun while you are on-stage. If you have fun, it is guaranteed they will have fun."

—Tony Walker

Wendy Reiss gets the audience involved in "follow the leader."

When using a game or activity, make sure you set the game up properly. Clearly explain the directions of the game and write them down on a flip chart or a handout, so that your audience will understand. Then GET INVOLVED YOURSELF. This will signal to the audience that they can let go and enjoy the activity.

Hatfields and McCoys

An example of the sort of activity you might use to energize a medium-sized group—and review material, as well—is an activity that David Freeborn calls the "Hatfields and McCoys." It's a question-and-answer game that works effectively to energize the audience and increase their retention. Divide the room into two equal groups. One group will be the Hatfields, the other the McCoys—and the presenter will be Da Judge. Da Judge will ask questions and each team will compete to answer.

There are only a couple of rules to the game. First, your audience members MUST jump to their feet and raise a hand to be recognized before giving an answer. Second, Da Judge is never wrong. A little friendly competition gets the room really going. You can keep score, play for prizes, or play just for the fun of it. Use your imagination! The key to Hatfields and McCoys, as with all games and activities, is to keep it brief enough to make your audience want to come back for more.

"Do It!" activity gets everyone involved.

A little friendly competition keeps everyone interested.

121

There are a couple other simple rules to keep in mind when designing games and activities.

1. Always choose an energizing activity.

2. Make sure the game relates to the point you're trying to illustrate.

3. Pacing is the name of the activity game. It's better to run a short, quick-moving game and have the audience return to their seats laughing and energized and wanting more than to draw out an activity and risk a loss of impact.

Speed Ball activity keeps the group energized.

Music

Nonverbal information is powerful to the eye—and to the ear. We spend a lot of time making sure that we signal our interest to audience members through careful body language, well-developed visuals, and so on. But we tend to neglect the other powerful sense at work during a presentation: hearing. The audience needs a break from your voice. And a good way to provide this is with music.

Music sets a mood, creates an atmosphere, and gives the audience's ears a special treat. Try to use different types of music

Secrets of the Pros

"When the number of awards is high, it makes the perceived possibility of winning something high as well. And then the average man will stretch to achieve."

—Tom Peters

"You are terrific" activity keeps the group involved.

for different effects. Take several types of CDs with you. Ask the audience what types of music they enjoy. The beginning and end of your presentation, as well as during breaks, are especially good times to use music.

Verbal Surveying

Keep your audience interested by keeping them involved! Don't *tell them* every key learning point. Ask the audience to *tell you* the key learning points after each exercise. This results in more participation, heightened credibility, and confirmation that they have indeed received the message. You want them to leave the session being impressed with how much *they* know, not how much *you* know. In

Ken Copeland and associates work to solve a team-building activity.

123

fact, several times during your
presentation you should get
general feedback by simply
surveying the audience out
loud. Ask them about the
pace of your presentation,
about how useful the content
is, even about the room temper-

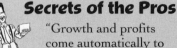

ature. The response will allow you to adjust as you make them the
most comfortable and, of course, the most able to really buy-in to
your message. Many people whom I watch present forget again
and again to get the audience members' feedback.

Stories and Anecdotes

Just as in real life, in a presentation stories create interest and add
spice to the day. While you should always leave room for stories and
anecdotes, audiences won't appreciate too many stories that are not
related to the topic. In general your stories should do one of three
things: illustrate a point, create humor, or relate your experience to
your audience's experiences. Also, allowing audience members to
tell their own stories is a good way to create rapport and audience
involvement. Remember, you always have time for a good story
that makes a point!

Some rules for using stories as business entertainment

➤ *Keep them short.* As I once heard a speaker say, "Don't tell me
where you bought the matches, just tell me how big the fire was."

➤ *Make them illustrate a point.* Audiences don't want to hear about
your generic experiences or observations. Relate the story to
some point you are making.

➤ *Use your own experience.* Whenever possible, your stories should
relate your own experiences rather than secondhand experience.
This makes the story immediate and credible.

Videos

We are an audiovisual culture and audiences respond to this type
of information. Use these tools! While you can only use so many

games, you can almost constantly use flip charts and posters. You can also regularly use videos. Remember, audiences retain up to 50 percent of what they see *and* hear, so videos and other audiovisual equipment add emphasis to your message. When using videos, enhance your audience's attention by taking a few minutes to set up what they're going to see. Give them a couple of hints about points to look for, or ask them to jot down two or three things they learned from the video. This will focus their attention and keep them actively involved as opposed to just passively watching.

For an in-depth outline of how to use video equipment and other tools of the presentation trade see chapter 9.

Taking Breaks

Breaks are also natural energizers. You can't take them every five to seven minutes (no matter how much audience members may wish you could) but you can have frequent breaks. To focus audience attention, keep the breaks short, or provide them with break activities—something to think or talk about and to be discussed when they return. You can also take breaks as opportunities to survey the audience and see what's working and what isn't. There are a few rules on breaks.

➤ Use frequent breaks, every 60 to 90 minutes.

➤ Be flexible on breaks—you may need them to be more or less frequent.

Is this sort of response from an audience member worth one buck to you? You bet it is!
Give away something, even if it is money.

➤ Know break logistics: where the restrooms are, what the smoking policy is, where the phones are, where the refreshments are.

➤ Create a break policy and let the audience know about it from the beginning.

➤ Manage breaks. Settle on a return time (e.g., "Let's return at 10:10 A.M.") rather than a length of time (such as, "Let's take ten minutes").

➤ Use gimmicks and prompts to alert audience members that breaks are ending (train whistle, music prompts, etc.).

Freebies

If it works at the beginning (see chapter 4) it will work in the middle. Give something away! I realized the great value of giving something away when I was giving a presentation in Denver with a partner. It was in the middle of a day-long presentation and we had covered all our morning material. Searching for something to divert our audience, my partner turned to a box of pens—something we were saving for later in our program. He started reviewing the morning's material by asking the audience random questions and tossing Bic™ pens around the room. The audience roared back to life! For the rest of the week we made sure we had pens for each new audience we saw.

Again, the items you give away don't have to be expensive, just unexpected and free. Below are a few good ideas for freebies you can carry with you.

➤ Pens, pins, ball caps, or other trinkets with an organization's name on it.

➤ Cassette tapes, videotapes, booklets of your own material, or that of others who might otherwise interest your audience. Always include your business card.

➤ Candy always works. Be careful to include a variety of chocolate and non-chocolate candies, as well as sugared and sugar-free, so everyone can participate.

Secrets of the Pros

"Give small gifts so that they will remember you."
—Dottie Walters

➤ Use a camera to take pictures of audience members engaged in activities, then give them copies of the photographs. They make nice presents, and it's something that they will always have to remind them of your presentation.

➤ Provide a simple handout summing up the major points of your talk.

➤ Money. Okay, call me simple. But I like to give away money, a dollar at a time. I have fifty fresh dollar bills gum-bound to a cardboard backing. I call them Texas Scratch Pads, and every time an audience member does something out of the ordinary—makes a humorous remark, adds value to the day, volunteers for an activity—he or she gets a buck. Audience members love this, and it's always worth the extra few dollars I spend.

Note taking

Note taking is an audience involver—especially if you have the time and resources to provide the audience with a note taker of some sort that is keyed to your presentation. Although we sometimes forget what we hear, retention soars when we reinforce it by writing it down. Take, for example, a shopping list. Even when we forget to take it with us, we often "see" what we wrote on the list. The act of writing "imprinted" the list in our memory.

I actually employ this in many of my train-the-trainer seminars. I call it the Very Important Point concept. Virtually all presentations contain too much information for the audience to readily absorb. So I ask my audiences to take notes—but notes with a twist. Rather than telling them what to write, I allow them to choose the material that seems important to them. Occasionally I review, just to prove to them how much they are picking up. When asking your audience to take notes, remember these rules:

1. *Suggest*, don't order, note taking. Try something like, "Here's an idea you might jot down."

2. Help attendees by sifting through the information. Ask that they only jot down the top three points that seem useful TO THEM.

3. Pause to give your audience time to take notes.

127

I often develop courses in which time is allowed for participants to break out into groups of two to seven people. I ask
each group to note on a flip chart what it believes are the best
points of the presentation. Then I have each group share its
very best points with the other groups.

One last note

The idea behind business entertainment is to keep even the most
reserved groups energized and interested. You should strive to
keep a fun, inviting, and risk-free environment during any activity
and the entire presentation. Make sure everyone gets and feels
involved. Remember, a little healthy competition and creative presenting go a long way. Keep your audiences interested by keeping
them entertained!

Very Important Points to Remember

✔ Audience members have an attention span of five to seven
minutes. Keep them hooked by giving them a jolt of business
entertainment at their natural attention lows.

✔ Audiences think faster than you can speak. Keep them occupied
by providing sources of input other than spoken words.

✔ Games and other energizers work best when they are well-
explained, quickly paced, and short.

✔ Everyone enjoys business entertainment, but be sure to tailor
your activities and diversions to the specific audience.

Fill in Your Favorite Tips from the Chapter

✔ _____
_____

✔ _____
_____

✔ _____
_____

This chapter reveals:

➤ How to view the room as a tool

➤ What types of visual aids are available and
the advantages and disadvantages of each

➤ How to select visual aids for YOUR presentation

➤ How to use tools like a pro

Using the Tools of the Trade

JEARY THEORY ━━━━━━━

To fully engage an audience and increase information retention, use as much variety as time and budget allow.

"Things seen are mightier than things heard."
—Alfred Lord Tennyson

The Scene ...

You want your presentation to make a great impact. And now you know that the greatest impact is made when people not only hear your words, but see them as well, and do it all in a comfortable atmosphere. There's a whole world of media out there—everything from flip charts and markers to overhead projectors, TVs and VCRs, and interactive computer equipment. What you need is a guide to sort through everything that's available and know what to use— and how and when to use it. Then you can make some decisions on how to add punch to your presentations.

The Solution ...

Turn to the handy toolbox on page 148. Presenters use dozens of tools in many different ways to enhance their message, ensure audience buy-in, and increase audience retention. Your only limitations are your own knowledge of the tools available and how to use them. After that, your imagination's the limit.

Secrets

1. **Tools are everywhere; know when and how to use them.**

2. **The room is the most overlooked tool a presenter has.**

3. **Visual aids: the secret to success**
   ➤ Why we use them
   ➤ When we use them
   ➤ How we use them

4. **Types of tools:**
   ➤ Flip charts
   ➤ Overhead and slide projectors
   ➤ Handouts
   ➤ TV/VCR (videos)
   ➤ Props
   ➤ Twenty-first-century tools: CDI and computers
   ➤ Presenter's toolbox

Tools

The New World Dictionary defines a tool as "any instrument or device necessary to one's profession or occupation." I would expand that to "any tool or device that makes one's occupation (or life, for that matter) a little easier and more effective." Like most trades, the presentation business has a lot of tools to master. Like any set of power tools, there are rules and guidelines for using them effectively. Before moving to the usual tools discussed in books on presentations, I'd like to spend some time on one of the most critical—and often overlooked—tools of the presentation trade.

The Room: The Most Overlooked of All Your Tools

Until now you might have taken the room for granted. After all, it's pretty much just a room, right? Wrong! The room is perhaps the single most important tool you have as a presenter. Inspiring an audience, as I have said repeatedly, means paying attention to every detail, however small or large. In the case of the room, we overlook it because it's too big for us to notice. Don't lose sight of the proverbial forest for the trees. The sooner you learn how to use the room to your benefit, the better.

Room Size

When it comes to rooms, the right size counts. A room that is too large makes the audience feel uneasy and lonely. It also places a lot of weight on your shoulders. You have to fill that void with lights, sound, and action. Likewise, a room that's too small makes for a cramped presentation. The right size is one in which everyone has room to relax in their seats and to get up and move around without bumping elbows. If you must choose one over the other, however, go for the slightly smaller room. Then at least your presentation seems well-attended and everyone gets to know everyone else.

➤ Make sure your room is the correct size for your audience.

➤ Make sure audience members are comfortable with the room.

➤ Large rooms and those with high ceilings are often cold and have a tendency to produce distracting echoes.

Room Shape

The shape of the room is important inasmuch as everyone must be able to see you, your visual aids, and, ideally, each other. Especially try to avoid:

➤ Rooms with structural supports that block the view.

➤ Rooms with deep recesses—unless people can sit there, it's a waste of space.

The Rules of the Room

Below is a summary of the rules and regulations for preparing and maintaining your room to create an inspiring presentation.

➤ When possible, select a room that is just right for the size of your audience. Keep in mind that too large is just as bad as too small.

➤ Rooms with high ceilings will echo and can be cold.

➤ Arrange your seating according to what you want to accomplish.

➤ Determine audio-visual requirements. Remember: everyone has to be able to see everything.

➤ Lighting is critical; know where all the lighting controls are and have a plan for using them.

➤ Know where heating and cooling controls are and who to call if you can't control them yourself.

➤ Familiarize yourself with how things work: window shades, microphones, etc.

➤ When possible use comfortable chairs.

➤ Regarding screens, monitors, and flip charts, consider their number, location, and size.

➤ When possible use a microphone for audiences of more than fifty participants.

➤ Decide whether you need a stage (or riser) in a hotel.

➤ If possible have the seating arrangement wide and flat rather than narrow and deep.

Once you have your room set up you'll be ready to fill it with the excitement and enthusiasm of your presentation. Make sure the room is ready and suited to your voice and the tools you will use to support it.

Secrets of the Pros

"I will form good habits and become their slave."
—Og Mandino

Windows

Natural lighting is terrific, but as a rule avoid windows. Why? Because you have enough to contend with keeping your audience's interest level at a high point without inviting them to look at the world as it passes by. Another problem is the sun—it constantly moves. This means that at some point during a morning-long presentation it will be shining in everyone's face. Nothing is more distracting and uncomfortable than having bright hot sunshine in your face while you're trying to listen—much less trying to speak. Also, the sun plays havoc with visual equipment, especially VCRs and television monitors, which can fade out if bright light falls on them.

If you have a room with windows, make sure you:

➤ Know where the rods and cords are for the blinds.

➤ Know how to open and close the windows.

➤ Arrange audience seating so that their backs are to the window.

➤ Rooms with many windows and no drapes: too much uncontrolled sun can kill a good presentation. It's bright, it's hot, and it moves, meaning it can bother everyone in the room throughout the day.

Room Seating

The seating arrangement for your room is critical. But too often presenters leave it to chance (or the evening set-up crew) to determine it for them. Don't leave your seating to chance. You want to create an inviting, comfortable environment. This means participants should have space enough to be comfortable and be able to move freely. They should be facing you and be able to see each other as much as possible.

There are generally three basic types of seating arrangements used for medium-size presentations:

➤ **Classroom Style:** in which participants sit four or more at straight tables (or just in chairs).

➤ **Rounds:** in which participants sit clustered at round tables.

➤ **U-Shaped:** where presenter is situated in the middle.

Classroom style ensures the audience will see you and that you'll see them. Rounds creates a feeling of camaraderie among participants and encourages interaction. The U-shape allows flexibility. In any case, make sure the audience members can see each other.

Examples of seating arrangements can be found on page 137.

Sound Systems, Lighting, and Other Miscellany

What might seem like small things to you will seem like big things to your audience. Busy as you are, you might overlook things like lighting, temperature, sound, and other factors that collectively contribute to audience comfort. Here are some guidelines to follow when considering these factors.

Sound System

Many hotel seminar rooms and office buildings have built-in sound systems if you intend to use music or other audio-visual media. I usually bring my own tape deck when I need audio support. However, if you do use on-site equipment, there are a few points to double-check.

➤ Sometimes the equipment doesn't work. Save yourself the embarrassment of finding this out in the middle of your presentation by checking everything beforehand.

➤ Make sure you know where the volume controls, on/off switches, and other such things are. ALWAYS preset volume controls before your audience arrives.

➤ Be sure that sound carries to all parts of the room. "Dead spots" can occur and can distract people from the message by making it difficult for them to hear.

Water/Refreshments

Whenever possible keep refreshments on hand either inside or just outside of the room. Otherwise your group will scatter in search of sustenance every time you break. Make sure your group won't have to bottleneck at the coffee table, and make sure there's enough refreshments on hand for everyone. It might not be your job. But it's your face they'll be looking at when the coffee runs out. And always make sure you have a glass of water for yourself. It's very hard to speak effectively with a dry mouth.

Temperature

The number-one environmental complaint about any presentation is temperature. You can never seem to please the whole room. Below are a few rules for keeping your room comfortable and temperate for your participants.

➤ Know where the temperature controls are.

➤ If you're in one of those hotels or schoolrooms where they lock the controls in a clear plastic box, make sure you know the person who has the key by name before your presentation starts. You'll be calling him or her at least once during the presentation.

➤ Arrive early and check the temperature. When a room is unused for a day or more, heat gets turned off in the winter and air-

Seating

▰▰▰ LARGE GROUPS ▰▰▰

```
                    0
X  X  X  X  X  X       X  X  X  X  X  X
X  X  X  X  X  X       X  X  X  X  X  X
X  X  X  X  X  X       X  X  X  X  X  X
X  X  X  X  X  X       X  X  X  X  X  X
X  X  X  X  X  X       X  X  X  X  X  X
X  X  X  X  X  X       X  X  X  X  X  X
X  X  X  X  X  X       X  X  X  X  X  X
```

▰▰▰ MEDIUM-SIZED GROUPS ▰▰▰

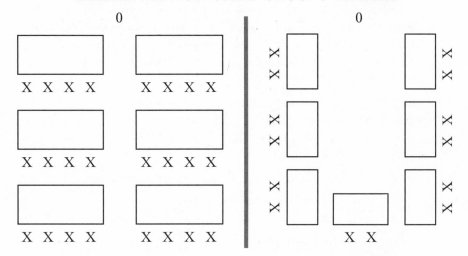

▰▰▰ SMALL GROUPS ▰▰▰

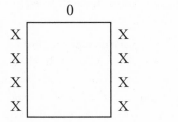

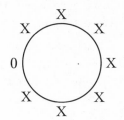

0 = Speaker
X = Participant

137

conditioning gets turned off in the summer. Show up early enough to get your room back to the right temperature if it has been unused for a day or so.

Electrical outlets/Light switches

You'll need both, so know where they are. The rule for lighting is this: full bright means high excitement. Keep the lights on as bright as possible throughout the entire presentation. If you must turn them down for projectors, see if you can turn off only a few of the lights. Then see if you have dimmers. If you must turn them down— always bring them back to full bright as soon as possible.

Visual Aids

Visual aids are the most common type of tool a presenter uses. Why? Because, pound for pound, they're the most effective thing in the room besides you for delivering your message and making your presentation inspiring. To paraphrase Confucius: A visual aid is worth a thousand words.

And recent research supports what Confucius figured out ages ago. People understand a message better when words are reinforced by pictures. In fact, here's a thumbnail sketch of what we know about audiences and visual aids.

➤ Different people receive different information in different ways.

  ➤ Auditorially—through their ears.

  ➤ Kinetically—through movement.

  ➤ Visually—through their eyes.

➤ Most people tend to be visually oriented when it comes to learning.

➤ Good visual aids get a point across in three to five seconds; words take three to five minutes.

Good visual aids reinforce, clarify, and drive points home. They are indispensable for introducing or summarizing ideas. They save time, hold people's attention, and help the audience focus its attention. They also give you a break. While the audience is focused on a videotape or slide projection, their eyes are away from you, giving you critical time to prepare the next section of your presentation, review notes, or just gather your thoughts.

Lindsay Lowe, Bob Meintrup, and Wendy Reiss use pre-prepared boards to help presentations run smoothly.

When to Use Common Visual Aids

Any time you wish to emphasize a point—really drive it home—make sure the audience sees it written out. Or better yet, *drawn* out, as in a picture. In general, there are about a half dozen instances when you must use some sort of visual support.

Use visual aids when you wish to:

➤ Increase retention

➤ Explain new concepts

➤ Summarize new concepts

➤ Present complex data such as statistics and graphs

➤ Get the audience to look at something other than the speaker

➤ Get the audience more involved

How to Use Common Visual Aids

The most common kinds of visual aids are:

➤ Flip charts

➤ Handouts

➤ Overhead projectors

➤ Slide projectors

➤ Props

➤ Videotapes and films

➤ High-tech video equipment

The DOs and DON'Ts for using the most common of these various visual aids are outlined below. But there are a few general rules and regulations to follow whenever you use any of them. With visuals there is one golden rule. AVOID THE DATA DUMP. Do not clutter the visual with information. The less words the better. Use pictures. Less is more. You get the idea.

Here are the rest of the rules for visual aids:

➤ *Keep visuals simple.* Ideally, keep to no more than five lines per page and five words per line on anything the audience has to read. Graphs should be simple, clean, and easy-to-understand. Never clutter a screen or a page.

➤ *Keep visuals legible.* Write slowly and clearly. Prepare everything you can on a computer or typewriter.

➤ *Keep visuals neat.* Written lines should be straight, graphs should be clear, and pictures should be centered.

➤ *Keep visuals consistent.* Your visual aids should appear to be uniform and consistent in their appearance.

➤ *Keep visuals unified.* Each page or screen should talk about one topic or idea. If you move on to something else, start a clean visual.

➤ *Use bulleted points and sentence fragments* (two- or three-word statements, usually without a verb) *instead of full sentences*. Sentence fragments are easier for audiences to absorb.

➤ *Use pictures instead of sentence fragments,* when possible. Pictures are even easier to understand.

➤ *Combine pictures, symbols, and key words* to create effective visuals.

➤ *Children's coloring books are a good source for pictures and drawings.* Use them to create overheads, pre-prepared flip charts and handouts.

➤ *Make visuals colorful.*

➤ *Use graphics related to the subject matter* that will help the audience retain key points.

Flip Charts

Flip charts are the most common visual aid around. They're easy-to-use, effective, and relatively inexpensive. That's not all that makes them great, either. I especially like the versatility of the flip chart. It's the Jeep of the presentation world—it can go anywhere and yet you still stay in control. You don't have to worry about finding an outlet, a bulb burning out, or dimming the lights to use a flip chart.

There are five main uses for flip charts:

1. Presenting information you wish to emphasize.
2. Focusing audience attention in one place.
3. Recording information—especially contributions from audience members.
4. Displaying what you've already covered.
5. Encouraging audience involvement.

In addition to the five main uses for flip charts, you should be familiar with the three types of flip charts at your disposal:

1. The pre-drawn flip chart. You prepare these flips before your audience arrives.
2. The preplanned flip chart. You plan these out and pencil in what you're going to write (audience members won't see the thin pencil marks), then trace over them in front of the audience.
3. The "on-the-fly" flip chart. You write these as you're moving along.

Although most presenters have used flip charts at some time in their lives, not many have ever bothered to learn how to use them correctly. The following pages give a few tips for using flip charts.

True inspiration comes when your audience:
- **Understands what you tell them**
- **Buys-in to the experience of listening to what you tell them**
- **Remembers what you tell them**

Visual aids are valuable because they facilitate all three of these levels.

Hot Tips for Cool Flips

➤ Use more than one flip chart whenever possible. Multiple flips give a feeling of energy and good planning.

➤ In general, fill in only the top three-fourths of your flip chart leaving the bottom one-fourth blank. This way even audience members in the back can see everything you write.

➤ Prepare as many flips as you can ahead of time. They look better and are easier to read. When preparing flips, leave every other page blank to absorb any ink that bleeds through.

➤ Use water-soluble markers rather than permanent ones—this will save your fingers from stains.

➤ Use scented markers—they don't have the strong chemical smell of permanent markers.

➤ Use a fat marker when printing. Placing the flat end of a fat marker on the paper makes anyone's printing look good!

➤ Use colors! The more colorful the better.

➤ Use darker colors—you can see these better.

➤ Draw a frame around the edge of the flipchart page for clarity.

➤ Use flipchart paper that has faint printed horizontal and vertical lines (graph paper). This makes it easier for you to keep your lines straight.

➤ Make sure every member of the audience can see the chart.

➤ Use an overhead to trace something on to a flip chart when you're preparing it.

➤ Post finished flips on the walls—this shows your audience how much material you're covering and "decorates" the room with a record of the presentation.

➤ Number your flip charts when you begin putting them on the wall.

➤ Have pre-torn strips of masking tape ready for posting the flips on the wall. You can stick the strips on the back of the flipchart stand *before* your presentation starts.

➤ Tear only one sheet at a time from the charts.

➤ When taking dictation from your audience, do your best to use their exact words—this makes audience members feel like pros.

➤ Always keep extra markers of all sizes and colors.

➤ Always consider the distance from your chart to the back row. If the back row has trouble seeing, consider using an overhead.

➤ Use pre-prepared flips to keep yourself on track.

Tony pre-prepares a flip chart.

➤ Solicit volunteer "scribes" from the audience to help you write things on flip charts. Audience members will enjoy the attention, and it'll save you from being distracted by writing as you speak.

The only real drawback to flip charts is their size. If the room or audience is too large, people near the back will have a difficult time seeing what you've written. For this reason, flip charts are best for small to medium groups (groups under one hundred people).

Flip charts are even more effective when the pages are taped up around the room.

Overheads and Slides

Overheads and slides work well for larger groups because they can be seen from everywhere in the room. Both are familiar to us in other settings: the overhead projector from school, the slide-show from our parents' vacation slides. Their biggest drawback, aside from the fact that you must rely on mechanical equipment which might fail, is the fact that you sometimes must darken the room. However, most modern equipment is designed to generate enough light so that you don't have to do this. Test your overheads and slides well before the audience members arrive.

Tips for Overheads and Slides

➤ Overheads should support your presentation not replace it.

➤ Use the 5x5 rule: aim to have no more than five points and five words per point on each transparency.

➤ When using an overhead, use a pointer.

➤ Don't hold the pointer on screen—it will shake and make you look nervous. Instead, move the pointer in a circular motion.

➤ Use sleeves to keep transparencies neat.

➤ Put notes in the margins if you use sleeves.

➤ Don't leave an "empty" white-light screen while you're talking. It's distracting to audience members.

Putting an overhead screen in the corner instead of the middle frees up space at the front of the room and keeps the presenter as the focal point.

➤ Create a cardboard "light-hood" to turn overheads on and off.

➤ Check for typos! They stand out in an overhead.

➤ When revealing steps, consider using overlays instead of cover-ups.

➤ Always carry a spare bulb; sooner or later you'll need it.

Denny Phelps prepares the night before a workshop.

➤ Carry a few blank transparencies.

➤ Whenever possible, place the screen right or left of the center of the room. Center stage belongs to the speaker.

➤ Always number your overheads in case they're dropped.

➤ If speaking about the overhead slide while you are moving, move in front of the overhead projector, not through the light.

➤ Use overhead markers to draw lines and circle key words to focus the presentation.

Handouts

Handouts, those sheets of paper you give to audience members periodically throughout the day, are useful for a number of reasons. First, they are something audience members can KEEP, making the presentation something they partly own. Second, they are about as versatile as flip charts but can hold more information. Of course, you don't want to overload them with information or participants won't read them. As with all visual aids, avoid the data dump. Fewer words work better!

➤ If time and budget allow, always use handouts!

➤ Here are six things to consider putting on handouts:

1. Statistics
2. Graphs
3. Examples

Secrets of the Pros

"If using multiple hand-outs, use different color paper for each one. Easier to refer to or back to (i.e., 'Let's look at the blue handout')."

—Alan Jones

4. Comparisons

5. Quotations

6. Expert testimonials

➤ Handouts need to match the sequence of the talk.

➤ Distribute handouts at the right time—too early or too late confuses the audience.

➤ When developing handouts, ask the question: "What information will people really want to take away?"

➤ Think about what the audience will actually DO with the handout.

➤ Keep handouts to a minimum to ensure their essential nature to the audience.

➤ When possible, use handouts that tie in with your other visuals.

➤ When possible, make sure your handouts have space for note taking.

➤ Use graphics and bulleted points. Avoid expository passages of text unless the handout is an essential reprint of a definitive article or story.

➤ Consider a summary handout.

➤ Number the pages so the audience can follow along.

➤ Keep it simple and clear—neatness counts.

➤ Always prepare extra handouts.

➤ Hole punch handouts.

➤ Consider making handouts the size your participants can use to put into binders, Daytimers, Franklin Planners, or other places where they keep important information.

➤ Organize all handouts ahead of time for quick distribution.

➤ If appropriate, have participant volunteers help distribute handouts (reward them at the end of the presentation with applause or a small prize).

Videos

Videos have pretty much replaced the film projector in the presentation business. If budget allows, you can develop sophisticated motion pictures at a relatively inexpensive cost. Videos are also good for recording previous presentations, testimonials, and other scenarios that might interest your audience. The biggest drawback is that unless you have a large screen, videos can be hard to see—especially when reading words on a screen. If you have an audience of more than twenty-five, you'll need two TV screens, one for each side of the room, which can become expensive and cumbersome.

In any case, if you wish to use video, you'll need a video cassette recorder (VCR) and a monitor or television for your presentations. You'll also need a video cart or a tall table to place them on. Presenters can use their own equipment or rent it. Video is a powerful aid, and one well worth mastering. Study the following points:

➤ Always check video equipment well in advance. A small problem detected early can save you embarrassment and time in the middle of your presentation.

➤ Preset volume levels by sitting in the last row and listening to see how well you can hear.

➤ Check picture quality the same way.

➤ Always cue your videotapes before using them.

➤ If you're making your own videotapes, leave space between segments so that you can cue them.

➤ If someone else is making the videotape, make sure you memorize or write out the sequence. Avoid surprises.

➤ Always carry a spare tape.

➤ Always carry spare cables.

Props

Props are visual aids in three dimensions. They are "the actual thing" you're talking about or a model of it. They work best when you're talking about complicated subjects that audience members actually need to see and feel. They're also entertaining. The biggest drawback to props is that you have to cart them around wherever you go and they can be expensive to create and replace. As a rule, if you use your imagination when creating them, you can save money. Here are a few tips:

➤ Be creative. Use common items that anyone can get their hands on.

➤ Be sure to display the prop long enough for everyone to get a good look.

➤ If possible, pass the prop around.

➤ Have duplicate props.

➤ Keep props in a bag or box to heighten excitement, then "reveal" them.

No, this isn't Bambi. It's a prop for a driving presentation.

Twenty-First-Century Presentations

Every day, new presentation tools are developed. Here is a short list of some of the other technology available to you:

➤ CDI: That's short for Compact Disk Interactive equipment. Like a VCR on CD, CDI gives the presenter mobility, a great picture, and most importantly, a level of interactivity and presentation flexibility previously unheard of.

➤ Presentation software: Companies are producing these regularly. Pop the program in your computer and you have terrific looking visuals you can shine on a screen.

TOOLBOX

There are a few tools that no presenter should leave home without. I carry mine around in a rolling airport suitcase that serves as a traveling presentations center and office for me wherever I go. You'll want to develop your own system, but below are the tools that I carry and suggest you make a part of your presenter's toolbox.

➤ A pointer of some kind—there are wooden pointers, retractable pointers that look like pens and extend like car antennas, and laser pointers that project a little red dot wherever you aim them

➤ Colored magic markers (scented)

➤ Scissors

Masking tape on the floor makes a great starting box for this activity.

➤ Extension cords

➤ Camera—Polaroids work best. You can take pictures of activities then give them away to audience members as freebies.

➤ Tape

- Masking tape for flips

- Transparent tape for handouts and miscellaneous uses

- Surgical tape which works as white-out for your flip charts and is very strong

➤ Push pins for hanging flip charts on cloth-covered walls that don't take tape

➤ An assortment of markers, pens, pencils, and scratch pads

➤ Breath mints—you'll be glad you took them

➤ Whistle—for high-energy fun

➤ Stopwatch—for keeping yourself on schedule and timing business entertainment activities for your participants

➤ Overhead markers—the type that you can wipe off from transparencies

➤ Aspirin—no headaches while presenting!

One Last Note

I've gone over many of the tools and aids you can use in your presentation, but don't let all this information overwhelm you. Select the tools that are right for your presentation and your personality. Part of developing and rehearsing your presentation is to plan which tools will work best. Practice makes perfect—the more you use the tools, the more comfortable you'll become. Always remember to rehearse with the props, flip charts, overheads, and other tools that you'll use on presentation day. And remember—the tools are there to make your job easier, not harder, and to increase your participants' enjoyment and retention. Use them accordingly and you'll be on your way to mastering the powerful tools of the presentation trade.

Very Important Points to Remember

✔ The room is a tool—become as familiar with each room you will present in as you are with all your other tools.

✔ Statistics show that we remember 20 percent of what we hear, 30 percent of what we see, and 50 percent of what we see *and* hear. Use visual aids!

✔ Visual aids:
  ➤ Increase retention
  ➤ Explain new concepts
  ➤ Summarize new concepts
  ➤ Present complex data such as statistics and graphs
  ➤ Get the audience to look at something other than the speaker
  ➤ Get the audience more involved

✔ Always check and double-check your tools. A little problem can become very big if you don't notice it until you're in the middle of your presentation.

✔ Know how to use the most common types of visual aids:
  ➤ Flip charts
  ➤ Handouts
  ➤ Overhead projectors
  ➤ Slide projectors
  ➤ Props
  ➤ Videotapes

✔ Develop an effective presenter's toolbox that works for you.
Then don't leave home without it!

Fill in Your Favorite Tips from the Chapter

✔ _____
_____

✔ _____
_____

✔ _____
_____

✔ _____
_____

This chapter reveals:

➤ How to manage your presentation

➤ How to ask for and use feedback from your audience

➤ How to handle questions and answers

10

Managing Your Presentation

JEARY THEORY ━━━━━━━━━

The most important part of managing your presentation is to relate the core of your talk to your audience Answer this question: What's in it for them?

"Your listeners won't care how much you know until they know how much you care."

— Anonymous

The Scene . . .

Your presentation seems to be going smoothly—no one has fallen asleep, no one has gotten up to leave—but you'd like to be sure things are working. Occasionally throughout the presentation, you ask the audience whether they have questions that need to be answered. You get some shaking of heads, a few shrugs, and a lot of silence. It could mean that you're doing such a good job that they understand everything—or it could mean they're totally lost. What you need is a simple system

Secrets of the Pros

"Say 'thank you' many times."

— Dottie Walters

153

for polling your audience to find out how the presentation is working and how to manage it better for them.

The Solution ...

Learn to use "Verbal Surveying" and "Targeted Polling" for obtaining honest, usable audience feedback. Audiences are full of information that will help you manage your presentation. Make sure you take advantage of it!

Secrets

1. Make sure there is a continual build of excitement from section to section. Learn to use business entertainment.

2. Use transitions between sections of your presentation.

   ➤ Introduce new material.

   ➤ Sum up before moving on.

3. Always give clear and simple directions.

4. Use Verbal Surveying to get feedback from the group.

5. Use Targeted Polling to get feedback from individuals.

6. Know how to handle questions and answer effectively.

Managing Your Presentations

Managing your presentation means mastering the mechanics of moving from section to section of your presentation. As I outlined in chapter 1, a presentation is not one long, uninterrupted talk. It is a group of related subsections that are strung together to present ideas and concepts to your audience. To this point, we've primarily dealt with how to develop, rehearse, and present those sections that make up the presentation. But running a smooth transition requires another skill—you have to be a good administrator as well. Making sure that you and your audience stay on track is one job many presenters neglect. In general, it requires you to have the following management skills:

➤ The ability to give clear, concise directions

➤ The ability to be decisive

➤ The ability to stick to a schedule

➤ The ability to remain flexible

➤ The ability to solicit and apply feedback from your audience

Audience Members

The best way to make sure your audience is maintaining interest and retaining information is to continually monitor them for response. Below I discuss "Verbal Surveying" and "Targeted Polling" as methods for gathering and interpreting audience response as the presentation moves along.

Rather than trying to survey the entire audience, pick two or three faces from the group and make these folks your audience barometers throughout the day. In chapter 2, I discussed four basic types of audience members: Prisoners, Vacationers, Graduates, and Students (see pp. 8–9 for a review of these audience-member profiles). Try to find a face from at least two of these groups. Note their attitudes at the beginning of the presentation, during the body of your presentation, and at the beginning of the first activity. Ask yourself these three questions:

1. What was their attitude when they got here?

2. What was their attitude when I began to speak?

3. How has their attitude changed?

Don't deliver your presentation to these people exclusively. You'll still want to concentrate on the entire room in order to make everyone feel they're part of the presentation. But by monitoring two or three faces consistently, you'll have a rough gauge on how your presentation is going.

Transitions

I mention transitions in this chapter because transitions are more than just the words or phrases you use to glue together different parts of your presentation. Transitions *do* glue the end of one section to the beginning of the next and provide a natural flow from one key point to another. But their most important job is to build interest.

Transitions Build Audience Interest

How? By building bridges from your presentation's key points. Many presenters spend hours and hours developing their presentations. More hours rehearsing, and even more hours getting the room ready. Then they negate all their work by failing to carefully build in and use transitions. Listening is hard work and the quickest way to lose track of an audience is by failing to tell them where you're going. Big mistake! Audience members need signals and guideposts on a regular basis, just like travelers do, to reassure them that they are on the right track and that it's worth continuing down this road. Transitions provide these mental guideposts in your presentation.

The general rule for transitions is this: Use one whenever you move from one major idea to another. It tells your audience that you've summed up idea one and are moving on to idea two. It doesn't have to be a lot of words—usually a sentence or two will do. But if I had to pick one problem many of the presenters I've coached and trained consistently exhibit, it is forgetting to use transitions. It's an easy mistake to make. You're excited, the audience is excited— who cares about something so small? The answer: your audience.

Bored faces are not necessarily a sign that you and your presentation are boring. Often it's just that your audience doesn't know where you are headed. Relate the core of your talk back to them by using the following rules on transitions:

➤ Use transitions between all important ideas you present.

➤ Use transitions to introduce and sum up new ideas, activities, or even before taking a break.

➤ Keep transitions short and sweet. They are the mortar, not the bricks, of your presentation.

➤ Use attention-getting statements, relative statistics, and humor.

➤ Vary your transitions.

➤ Use gestures and body movements.

Here are a few examples of transitions:

➤ This sums up what we need to understand about A; now let's look at B.

➤ In the next hour I plan to show you X, Y, and Z.

➤ Not only do these numbers show the problem, if we look at them closely, they reveal the solution.

Use your imagination and remember: Transitions are there to keep your audience interested, to join one of your ideas to another, and, most importantly, to provide your audience with important guideposts to keep them on track. Use them!

Giving Directions

Closely related to providing transitions is giving directions. Again, directions serve as guideposts to your audience and cut down on confusion. Your audience will be feeling four tensions (see chapter 4)—there is tension among themselves, between them and you, between them and their materials, and between them and their environment. The reason they feel these tensions is because they are unsure of what to expect.

Whenever you ask your audience to do something—whether it is simply to jot down an idea or take a break—give them an absolutely clear idea of what they have to do. Put yourself in their shoes. They don't know what you want, and they don't know your personality. Will this presenter embarrass me if I make a mistake or come back late? Confusion is a close cousin to boredom—and

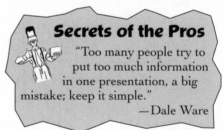

Secrets of the Pros

"Too many people try to put too much information in one presentation, a big mistake; keep it simple."
—Dale Ware

both are deadly to your presentation. Whenever you set up an activity or give the audience any other set of instructions, invest in the extra two minutes it takes to give clear instructions.

Here are some rules for clear instructions:

➤ Have instructions for activities, breaks, using materials, or anything else requiring audience participation planned out in advance of the presentation.

➤ Break your instructions into clear, briefly defined steps.

➤ Try to keep these points to a few in number. Anything more than five steps will confuse the audience.

➤ When you arrive at the point in your presentation where instructions are needed, announce to the audience, "I have a few simple steps for doing this activity."

➤ Write the steps out in brief bulleted points on a flip chart so audience members can look up to make sure they're on the right track.

➤ Be prepared to answer questions about your instructions.

A little time spent giving clear instructions will save a lot of time later trying to unravel confusion and getting your audience back on track. Audience members appreciate clear instructions. Your presentation will run more smoothly and your ideas and activities will become much more effective when your audience knows exactly what you want.

Secrets of the Pros

"Tell me about it ..."
—Dottie Walters

The Audience: Verbal Surveying

Verbal Surveying is a method for making sure that the entire room is benefiting from the presentation. Audiences rarely complain, which often means they are quietly putting up with something that is annoying them, distracting them, or otherwise occupying their attention and hurting your presentation. Rather than passively waiting for the audience to give you information on things like room temperature, the pace of your presentation, or even the difficulty of the content, become proactive by verbally surveying the room. Also take advantage of breaks and activity time to ask

Tony does a verbal survey.

158

quality-control questions of random audience members. Cover such topics as:

➤ Your audience's comfort—temperature, their ability to hear and see clearly

➤ The quality of your content

➤ The pace of your presentation—too slow or too fast?

➤ Whether your audience is being entertained

➤ Whether they are retaining the material you're presenting

If audience members admit something isn't going correctly, fix it! Otherwise you've wasted your time and hurt your credibility. Above all, don't take criticism personally. View it as an opportunity to make your presentation even better!

John Bacon works both sides of the room.

Individuals: "Targeted Polling"

Targeted polling is similar to verbal surveying, except you select a few individuals and ask them questions throughout the presentation. Select two or three individuals from the group very near the beginning. Keep an eye on how they respond to your material, occasionally asking them specific questions about specific parts of your presentation. Choosing a few people to monitor the course of the presentation will give you an idea of how the presentation is developing for each of the participants.

You can really take advantage of one-on-one targeted polling during breaks and/or lunch time. Choose an individual you'd like feedback from and talk with them at the break. Get them to open up and give you suggestions. They would love the one-on-one attention and often become champions for you in the big picture. People love to give suggestions and opinions. As a presenter, you should love to know what your audience is thinking.

159

What's in It for Me?

The most important thing you can do to manage your presentation and make sure it runs smoothly is to put yourself in your audience's shoes and continually ask yourself this question: What's in it for me? Every participant needs a reason to listen to what you are saying. It's not enough to explain what some concept, idea, behavior, product, or anything else *is* or how it works. To interest an audience, you have to drive your message home by telling them WHAT IT DOES FOR THEM.

From the minute you begin designing your presentation to the moment you close it, be aware of the reasons your audience will have to listen. Continually relate your talk back to these reasons. Everyone wants something, and some good motivators are:

> **Secrets of the Pros**
>
> "We all have a story to tell, and people want to hear that story. Tell your story well, with a high level of energy, and you will always have an audience willing to listen."
> —Frank Walker

➤ material gain

➤ fame

➤ respect

➤ glory

➤ prestige

➤ self-advancement

➤ approval

➤ peace of mind

Make sure you're delivering something your audience needs and wants. It's what you're there to do. Do it well and regularly, and your audience will respond.

Work the Whole Room

It almost goes without saying, but don't be like one of those teachers who favors a few students over all the rest. Make sure that in your presentation you work the entire room. Working the room means making sure every audience member is engaged and feels involved and feels some reason to continue listening to you.

> **Make your presentation meaningful to the audience by getting your audience physically involved and tie all key points to their needs. All audiences are asking this question: what's in it for me? A skydiver will not become bored learning to pack her own parachute. Her reward for learning the skill is too important.**
> **—Myra Ketterman**

You can maintain contact with the whole room by:

➤ Moving. Don't stand in one place.

➤ Maintaining eye contact. Look everyone in the eye for a few moments on a regular basis.

➤ Walking into your audience. Don't stand behind a podium or lectern if you can help it. Move through the audience.

I also ask people to smile when we start. For example, when I ask someone to write something down I ask them to look at me *and smile* when they've finished. I acknowledge each of them as they look up, have eye contact with everyone in the room, and let them drive the activity. Work the room!

Answering Questions: How to Avoid Getting Tripped Up

The question of questions—when to ask for them and how to answer them—is important, and we'll address it fully a little later. However, questions at the early stage of a presentation, at that point when you're letting the audience in on your objectives and getting them to buy-in to the day, raise special issues. At this stage of the game there will be three basic kinds of questions to watch out for. They are:

1. **What-does-it-all-mean** questions. These require a long-winded answer which you don't want to provide this early in your presentation.

2. **When-will-we . . .** questions. These should be answered within the normal course of the presentation.

3. **Who-do-you-think-you-are** questions. These questions are often hostile. The intent is to test your authority.

161

Although the first two are a little easier than the third, in general these are all types of questions to void and deal with swiftly when they occur. Question type 1 requires a *parent's* skill and can usually be answered with a simple, "That's a question we don't have time to answer right now, but we'll discuss where you might find the answer at break." Type 2 requires a *teacher's* skill. "We'll be covering that topic in a few minutes," will usually do. Type 3 requires the subtle, tough skills of a *coach*—you've got to prove yourself and neutralize the negative question. The trick here is to: a) rephrase the question in your own words, and b) provide an answer that avoids arrogance and keeps you looking dignified. For example, someone might ask, "What's the value of my being here?" Your answer might be, "We're going to cover some points that are designed to make your life a little easier—and you might even have some fun doing it."

In general, there are three basic mistakes made when unexpected questions are asked:

1. Answering too soon

2. Answering too much

3. Creating a pointless dialogue with one person

The key to avoid getting tripped up is to expect the unexpected question. This doesn't mean knowing what the question will be but having a ready method to meet any question. The following tips will help you prepare for questions beforehand and give you direction on how to handle questions when they come up in your presentation:

1. Brainstorm possible questions during your preparation.

2. Write out these questions and their answers on a 3x5 card.

3. Practice responding to questions with an associate.

4. When an audience member asks a question, ALWAYS repeat the question to make sure everyone hears it. This makes the audience member feel as if the question was intelligent, and it also gives you time to think.

5. Listen to the whole question. Don't interrupt a question, don't make fun of a question, and never finish a question from an audience member.

6. Involve the whole audience with your answer. Ask for audience members to provide input.

7. Don't get stuck in a dialogue that will bore the room. Tell the questioner you'll see him during a break or after the talk.

8. When someone asks a question, make sure you understand the question before answering.

9. For confusing questions, get a better understanding of the question by asking for clarification. Don't try to answer a question you don't fully understand.

10. Facilitate the questioning—bounce questions back to the audience to get them thinking.

11. Pause a moment when someone asks you a question. This makes you look serious and gives you time to think.

12. Learn the art of bridging. Refocus the question in a way that connects the listener's question with the point you're trying to make.

13. Don't guess if you don't know.

14. Don't allow one or two participants to dominate the questioning.

15. Give answers everyone can understand.

16. Practice and rehearse your answers.

17. You don't have to know all the answers! But you do need to always address the questions.

18. Anticipate and rehearse possible questions prior to the presentation.

19. Never close your presentation with a question-and-answer period. It can raise doubts and undo your presentation. Take questions well before you close.

Questions are your chance to show the room your knowledge *and* your honesty. Don't fake an answer. The willingness to help find the *correct* answer will impress a room more than the willingness to give any answer, even an incorrect one.

Very Important Points to Remember

✔ Managing your audience means seeing things from their points of view. Strive to make your presentation work for them.

✔ A confused audience is difficult to manage. Always sum up and use transitions before moving on to keep audience members aware of where the presentation is moving.

✔ Whenever you ask the audience to do something, make sure you give clear instructions. Write the instructions out on a flip chart so audience members can refer back to them.

✔ To get feedback and gauge your audience's response to your presentation, use Verbal Surveying and Targeted Polling.

✔ Know how to answer questions; a skilled handler of questions builds audience trust.

Fill in Your Favorite Tips from the Chapter

✔ _____

_____

✔ _____

_____

✔ _____

_____

✔ _____

_____

PART 4
Closing Your Presentation

This chapter reveals:

➤ The difference between summarizing and closing

➤ How and why to summarize throughout the day

➤ How to use summarizing to set up a terrific ending

Summarizing

Summarizing

"It's what you learn after you know it all that counts."
—John Wooden

The Scene . . .

Your presentation has been a full day long. You've covered a ton
of material and you need to make sure your audience takes away
a few very important points to ensure that your words become
action—but how?

The Solution . . .

Use effective summarizing—both throughout the day and in the
end. Part of the Jeary Theory for giving presentations is that you
should get the audience to tell you what you're going to tell them,
let them tell you what you're telling them (verbal surveying and
targeted polling) and finally, get them to tell you what you've told

them. Summarizing effectively allows you to accomplish that third and most important step for driving your information home.

Secrets

1. Summarize throughout the day.
2. At the conclusion, link the closing back to the introduction.
3. Before going into your close, summarize all the main points and tie the presentation together.
4. Prove you've met your and your audience's objectives.
5. Your audience needs closure before you conclude.
6. Focus the presentation.
7. Keep it short.

Summarize Throughout the Day

One thing many presenters neglect to do is create clear, effective summaries. This mistake is easy to make. After all, you understand the information you're presenting very well—you don't really need to summarize it for yourself. You're more interested in moving swiftly from point to point. Isn't that better than slowing down at the risk of boring your participants by rehashing what's already been covered? The answer is a resounding NO! You will not bore your audience members by summarizing points. You will, however, accomplish three important things:

1. You'll keep your audience focused and let them know where they've been, which is the best way to let them know where they're heading.
2. You'll increase your audience's retention rate by summarizing exactly what's important about what you've told them.
3. You'll heighten the audience's interest by reducing confusion.

The key to effective summarizing at the *close* of your presentation is to summarize *throughout the day*. Each time you conclude an activity or a segment of your presentation that includes a key point, make sure you summarize it for the audience. There's a simple formula for doing this.

1. Introduce key point

2. Explain it

3. Discuss it and engage in activities

4. Recap key point

5. Give a transition

6. Introduce new key point

Once you establish this dynamic, the audience will find it easy to follow you and they'll trust what you have to say. When you summarize, be sure to do the following:

➤ Always signal to the audience that you are summarizing points.

➤ Ask them what THEY think the main points are—they'll retain what they say better than if they hear it from you.

➤ Write THEIR answers on a flip chart.

➤ Add any point that they didn't include.

When summarizing, keep it short, simple, and clear. Your summaries should last *no more than one or two minutes*. Know ahead of time what three points will sum up any of your key ideas, statements, etc. An audience receives a blizzard of information, even in the shortest presentation. Summarizing helps them understand what's really important!

Summarizing throughout the presentation has an added benefit. It gives you and your audience the practice you'll need to summarize just before you close the presentation. Continuous summarization prepares the audience intellectually *and* emotionally for the close. Remember, there's a difference between closing and summarizing:

➤ SUMMARIZING drives your points home intellectually for the audience. It also prepares them emotionally for your close.

➤ CLOSING allows you to emotionally motivate your audience to act on everything that has come before.

The End of Your Presentation

Audience members, like all other people, think with their rational mind, but usually act upon emotion. While it is important to motivate

169

your audience emotionally at the end of the presentation, you still can't skip the rational intellectual part. This is what summarizing at the end of your presentation does.

Too often even experienced presenters want to rush from their last major point into a big, emotional close. But doing so leaves out a crucial step—the summary. Unless you remember to summarize the main points from your presentation, your audience will lack closure and will not be fully inspired to act upon your words.

When you come to the end of the material you have presented, take a moment to reiterate your opening statement. This will link the end of the presentation back to your early points and begin the process of closure for your audience.

Very Important Points

You'll notice that at the end of each chapter I've included "Very Important Points to Remember." I have also used the VIP concept in major training initiatives. A few years ago I realized that almost every presentation has too many points for an audience to remember. If you don't provide closure point by point, and if you don't wrap up the presentation by providing the closure a summary delivers, your audience won't know what to take away.

To solve the problem I use the VIP method. Participants in many of my seminars receive a booklet called a "VIP note taker," where *they* can write down the points they found most important. At the end of each segment, I ask for a few examples of important points from participants. Not only does this engage them, it also creates audience buy-in because *they* are in control of what is important. The VIP method:

➤ Increases retention

➤ Increases audience buy-in

➤ Puts audience members in charge

➤ Makes audience members the heroes

Try the VIP method next time *you* give a presentation!

The opening and the closing are the most important parts of your presentation. When summing up at the end of the day, you want to bring the former into your audience's mind and prepare them for the latter. Just as meeting and greeting is a critical set-up for your opening, so effective summarizing is the critical set-up for your close. An effective summary ties the presentation together and allows you to create the set-up for your emotional close.

Prove You've Met Your Objectives and Your Audience's Expectations

Once you've tied the end to the beginning, the next step of summarizing is to prove you've met your objectives. By reviewing these objectives, you give the audience a clear idea of what you've been over. At this stage you will also want to review the main points of the day. Prepare handouts or an overhead for doing so. This will create a sort of "high-points" review for the audience and remind them of what has been important throughout the day.

At the beginning you asked your audience for their expectations of the day and you wrote them down on a flip chart. Now is the time for the payoff. Return your audience's attention to the flip chart and go through them, one by one, ensuring that you met or exceeded those expectations. Since your audience helped create the list, you will already have them on your side. They'll see in seconds that you delivered what you promised.

Focus the Presentation

Your summary should bring all the various ideas and images of your presentation into sharp focus. Here are the basic steps to delivering an effective summary:

1. Let your audience know you are summarizing the points of the presentation—and ask what they believe were the major points.

2. Review your objectives from the opening to let them know you achieved them.

3. Review their expectations from the beginning of the presentation to let them know you met them.

4. Keep your summary short. It should take no more than five minutes. Anything longer will begin to seem redundant and unnecessary.

171

5. Include your audience. If they say it was important—it was!

Remember, your audience needs closure before they move into the real closing. Deliver this by taking a few minutes to sum up the presentation.

Very Important Points to Remember

✔ Summarizing and closing are two different things.

✔ Summarizing ties the themes of the presentation together and creates intellectual buy-in for audience members.

✔ Closing (see chapter 12) creates emotional buy in and inspires the audience to act upon your words.

✔ Effective summarizing means tying the end of your presentation back to the beginning of your presentation.

✔ Effective summarizing means proving you've met your objectives *and* the audience's expectations.

✔ Effective summarizing means clearly reviewing the most important concepts of the day and what they mean for your audience.

✔ An effective summary provides closure for the presentation's information and sets up a powerful closing.

Fill in Your Favorite Tips from the Chapter

✔ _____

_____

✔ _____

_____

✔ _____

_____

✔ _____

_____

This chapter reveals:

➤ How to close after you've summarized

➤ How to use emotion to ensure audience buy-in

➤ What to avoid when closing

12

Close It Right!

JEARY THEORY ▬▬▬▬▬▬

A fine closing will make them feel good about what they've learned, inspire them to act, and leave them with something by which to remember you and your key message.

"Great is the art of beginning; but greater is the art of ending."

—Henry Wadsworth Longfellow

Secrets

1. Use emotion in your close.

2. Always include a call to action.

3. Try to invoke a future challenge.

4. Go over next steps.

5. Closing killers:

   ➤ Q&A

   ➤ Apologizing

➤ Admitting that you missed something

➤ Skipping the summary

➤ Rambling on

Saying Goodbye

Your presentation should end with a bang! The best openings are attention-grabbers. The same is true of closes, so many of the same techniques can be used. Some, of course, will be more appropriate than others, but all of them should solidify the common ground you've been covering from the beginning of your presentation.

Some good attention-grabbers for closings are:

➤ Questions that challenge participants and leave them pondering a course of action

➤ Quotations that form the basis for a rhetorical closing question

➤ A personal anecdote that illustrates the points made in the talk

➤ A slice-of-life story that illustrates the ending of your presentation

➤ An analogy that brings the main points of your presentation together

These "attention-grabbers" function as transitions to prepare the audience to leave your presentation. Once you've gotten your audience's attention, you need to give them a reason for believing the words they've heard and, more importantly, you need to inspire them to act on those words.

Appeal to Emotion

Closing is much more than merely bringing your presentation to an end, though many presenters do little more than stop talking at the end of their presentation. The close is the last—and luckily the most powerful—opportunity to inspire your audience. Think of summarizing and closing as a one-two punch. In the summary you've set the stage by reaffirming value to the audience while setting them up for the emotional punch of the close.

By emotion I mean that you should appeal to what is human in your audience. Just like any great symphony or play, the final stanza of a presentation should tie together all that led to the end before delivering an emotional punch. By this stage of the presentation, you should have covered everything that appeals to the audience's rational mind. Now it's time to appeal to emotion and get them to act.

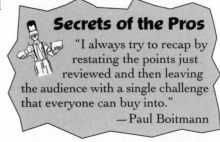

Secrets of the Pros

"I always try to recap by restating the points just reviewed and then leaving the audience with a single challenge that everyone can buy into."
—Paul Boitmann

These are some basic rules for any close:

➤ APPEAL TO EMOTION: Your audience thinks with their rational mind but acts on emotion.

➤ Keep it short: The close itself should last no more than TWO MINUTES. Anything longer and the emotional power will turn syrupy.

➤ Be positive: Never discuss negatives.

➤ Be motivational: Assure your audience that their actions do matter.

➤ Be energetic: Your energy and enthusiasm will inspire the audience more than anything you have to say. If the last thing they see is your enthusiasm, they will leave feeling enthusiastic and ready to act.

Prepare Your Ending

It's a good idea to have a clear picture of your close before you get there. By this stage everything should be done. The worst ending is an ending that simply ends: "Well, I guess that's about it, any questions?" You can avoid this poor ending by knowing what you will say at the end and saying it with emotion. To determine what direction your close should take, ask yourself the following questions:

➤ What does my audience want?

➤ What objections will my audience have to putting my message into action?

➤ How strong a case have I made?

➤ What are the next steps my audience must take to act on my presentation?

An appeal to the emotions of your audience requires that you be on common emotional ground to start with, since your appeal relies upon the assumption of common beliefs and feelings. This is true for even the stuffiest audiences. The chairman of a company fighting a takeover bid, for example, may call on company loyalty and history to urge stockholders to reject the tendered offer. Emotion is always *appropriate, provided you consider the type of audience you have and what their needs are.*

That Warm and Fuzzy Feeling

The close is literally your last word to the audience. Make the most of it by keeping it short and making sure it's something that will inspire the audience to act. Here are some examples:

1. **Quotations:** You can find quotations on almost any subject under the sun in sourcebooks for speakers and similar books.

Appealing to his audience to speak out in defense of their beliefs, Washington state's licensing director, R. Y. Woodhouse, closed with a story told by a minister during the Holocaust:

"... They came first for the Communists, and I didn't speak up because I wasn't a Communist.

"Then they came for the Jews, and I didn't speak up because I wasn't a Jew.

"Then they came for the trade unionists, and I didn't speak up because I wasn't a trade unionist.

"Then they came for the Catholics, and I didn't speak up because I was a Protestant.

"Then they came for me, and by that time no one was left to speak."

His appeal was largely emotional. But it was also dignified and, in the end, extremely powerful.

2. **Stories:** Stories are good when you need to make a point and drive it home with emotion. These types of stories are especially effective:

   ➤ Success stories

   ➤ Rags-to-riches stories

   ➤ Depression-to-elation stories

   ➤ Defeat-to-victory stories

3. **Calls to action:** Audiences need to be reminded that words only matter when they lead to ACTION. It works for great military leaders, why not try it for yourself? Challenge your audience to action. It's an emotionally effective and satisfying way to end your presentation—for them and for you.

4. **Next steps:** Cover the next steps with the audience—those things they can do to actually put words into actions that will benefit them.

Closing Killers

Here are some things to avoid at all costs:

➤ Conducting questions and answers at the end of your presentation: This is the single most common—and unfortunately most devastating—way to close. It moves the audience's focus from your message, introduces doubts, and lasts for an indefinite length of time. The right place to solicit questions and answers is just before you go into your summary (see chapter 11).

➤ Apologizing: Don't apologize throughout the presentation, but if you must apologize, never do it at the end.

➤ Admitting something was missed: It's too late now to go back. Why admit you missed something? Move on.

➤ Skipping the summary: This leaves the audience dangling and instead of ending with a warm and fuzzy feeling you get only the fuzzy.

➤ Rambling: Your close should be short and sweet—anything longer than two minutes will stop being emotional and become sappy. Keep it short.

Avoid the previous mistakes like the plague and you'll be guaranteed to avoid disaster!

The Send-Off

Your farewell should be as enthusiastic as your welcome. Always include some farewell in your close. Often, your audience will applaud. Accept it graciously and with a smile. Audiences have a need to give applause—who are you to stop them? Make sure you do three things at the very end:

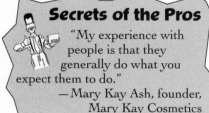

Secrets of the Pros

"My experience with people is that they generally do what you expect them to do."
—Mary Kay Ash, founder, Mary Kay Cosmetics

1. Thank the audience for their time and participation.

2. Say goodbye!

3. Remain available until ALL audience members have left.

This last point is very important, yet often overlooked. Audience members may want to speak to you after your talk. NEVER deny them this opportunity. You should remain as enthusiastic then as you have been throughout the talk. Many a presenter has succeeded in creating a terrific presentation and a perfect close only to undo it

John Davis catches negative thinking where it belongs, in the trash. A high-impact activity that receives great response.

A farewell photo on a plaque makes a great closing gift.

all by making him or herself inaccessible to the audience afterward. Allow your audience to speak with you, ask questions, and thank you after you're done. You are on stage until you're back at home!

Congratulations!

You have reached the end of your presentation—and almost the end of the book. Follow its advice, study the concepts, and use it for a handy reference guide and your skills as a presenter will increase. In fact, if you turn to the next short chapter, you'll get some tips and pointers on how to improve continuously.

Very Important Points to Remember

✔ Emotion means appealing to what is human in your audience.

✔ Audiences think with their intellect but act upon emotion.

✔ Use an attention-grabber to let the audience know the end is near.

✔ Keep the closing brief—no more than two minutes, otherwise the emotion will become sappy.

✔ Always include a farewell at the very end of the presentation.

✔ Remain accessible to the audience until every member has left.

Fill in Your Favorite Tips from the Chapter

✔ _____

_____

✔ _____

_____

✔ _____

_____

✔ _____

_____

This chapter reveals:

➤ How to improve your skills as a presenter

➤ How you, your audience and others can help you

➤ Valuable reference information for more study

13

Continuous Improvement

"The trouble with most of us is that we would rather be ruined by praise than saved by criticism."

—Dr. Norman Vincent Peale

Improving Your Skills

If you simply follow the tips and apply the concepts laid out in this book, you will become a more effective presenter. Guaranteed. But if you're like me, you'll want to continuously improve. Presenting is like anything else—practice makes perfect. The key is in practicing effectively. This chapter briefly outlines what you can do to help yourself improve, and how your audience and others can help you as well. Also in addition, I include a reference guide that includes periodicals, books, and even trainers in your area who can help you improve your skills at presenting.

Secrets of the Pros

"Success is not a doorway, it's a stairway."

—Dottie Walters

What You Can Do

The first step is a commitment toward continuous improvement. That means going after as many opportunities to present as you can and rehearsing continually to improve your skills. It also means seeking and *listening* to constructive criticism. You make or break presentations with details. There's always some tweak you can make, some small something you can improve on. Become dedicated to the process!

You can do self-evaluations in any combination of the following ways:

➤ Rehearse with a tape recorder or, better yet, a videotape. If you get into this habit, you will eliminate surprises from your own presentations.

➤ Always consider new ways to accomplish the same job. Experiment!

➤ Present your next (or last) presentation in front of a mirror; then for a couple of friends; then to a large group. This will give you a feel for how different presenting before different sized groups can be.

➤ Fix *any* flaws—however small—before the next presentation.

Be imaginative when it comes to improving yourself. Perhaps the most powerful tool of everything discussed so far is the videotape. You may be the last person to know you're making a mistake. But to see yourself doing it over and over again is a sure way to stop repeated mistakes.

Audience Evaluations

Audience evaluations are useful tools for improving your performance and for gauging how effective a particular presentation has been. Additionally, these evaluations result in very detailed information from the mind that matters most—that of the participant. Videotapes are powerful for

> **Secrets of the Pros**
>
> "The only true security in life comes from knowing that every single day you are improving yourself in some way."
>
> —Anthony Robbins

revealing the big picture, but audience evaluations provide a much more exacting level of detail. For optimal results, you have to develop a detailed checklist of specifics and ask your audience's opinion. You'll want the checklist to be:

➤ Easy to use

➤ Specific

➤ Honest

➤ Comprehensive

➤ As brief as possible

Secrets of the Pros

"Don't wish it were easier, wish you were better."
—Jim Rohn

As a rule, your forms should be no more than one page and should solicit information from a number of different areas of the presentation including:

➤ The topics and content of the presentation

➤ The presenter's performance and preparation

➤ The materials used

➤ The effectiveness of visual aids

➤ Areas that need improvement.

➤ Participation

You can use a checklist format or a 1–10 evaluative or short-answer format. The object is to get as detailed a critique as possible from the audience. (Some sample evaluation forms follow on the next three pages, and I've repeated the forms in the appendix in the back of this book so you can remove them for photocopying.)

Secrets of the Pros

"Struggling is not a comfortable thing. It involves long hours of work."
—Harvey Mackay

Prepare yourself. Audiences can be tough critics and even one tough review in a hundred will sting. But it will also help you improve. We're after 100 percent buy-in. When reviewing evaluations, remember three very important rules.

➤ The audience is always right.

➤ The audience is always right.

➤ The audience is always right.

187

PRESENTATION ASSESSMENT

Skill/Traits	1	2	3	4	5	6	7	8	9	10

Preparation:

Analyzing audience — — — — — — — — — —

Developing objectives — — — — — — — — — —

Developing visual aids — — — — — — — — — —

Checking logistics — — — — — — — — — —

Overcoming nervousness — — — — — — — — — —

Stating main ideas — — — — — — — — — —

Deciding supporting
information — — — — — — — — — —

Creating an opener — — — — — — — — — —

Developing transitions — — — — — — — — — —

Structuring the main body — — — — — — — — — —

Using visual aids — — — — — — — — — —

Preparing the close — — — — — — — — — —

Delivery:

Vocal image

Volume — — — — — — — — — —

Pace — — — — — — — — — —

Pausing — — — — — — — — — —

Verbal image

Vocabulary — — — — — — — — — —

Grammar — — — — — — — — — —

Pronunciation — — — — — — — — — —

Visual image

Dress/Appearance — — — — — — — — — —

Posture — — — — — — — — — —

Gestures — — — — — — — — — —

Eye contact — — — — — — — — — —

Facial expressions/Smile — — — — — — — — — —

Challenging situations:

Handling questions — — — — — — — — — —

Managing mishaps — — — — — — — — — —

Controlling problem people — — — — — — — — — —

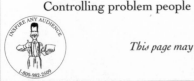

This page may be reproduced without permission.

BODY LANGUAGE EVALUATION

Title _____ Name of Evaluator _____ Date _____

NOTE TO THE EVALUATOR: In this presentation the speaker is concentrating on body language. He or she should use gestures, facial expressions, and other body movements that illustrate and enhance the verbal message. In evaluating this speech, focus on delivery rather than content. Use a rating scale of 1 to 10, where 1 represents unsatisfactory and 10 indicates outstanding.

Action	Rating	Comments
Preparation	1 2 3 4 5 6 7 8 9 10	_____
Organization	1 2 3 4 5 6 7 8 9 10	_____
Appearance	1 2 3 4 5 6 7 8 9 10	_____
Topic	1 2 3 4 5 6 7 8 9 10	_____
Manner	1 2 3 4 5 6 7 8 9 10	_____
Body movements	1 2 3 4 5 6 7 8 9 10	_____
Posture	1 2 3 4 5 6 7 8 9 10	_____
Gestures	1 2 3 4 5 6 7 8 9 10	_____
Eye contact	1 2 3 4 5 6 7 8 9 10	_____
Facial expressions	1 2 3 4 5 6 7 8 9 10	_____

This page may be reproduced without permission.

POST-PRESENTATION EVALUATION

Instructions: Read each group and circle the number that most closely describes how effective the presentation was in each respective area. Use a rating scale of 1 to 10 in which 1 represents unsatisfactory and 10 indicates outstanding.

Preparation and Content

1. Opening   1   2   3   4   5   6   7   8   9   10
2. Content material   1   2   3   4   5   6   7   8   9   10
3. Organization of material   1   2   3   4   5   6   7   8   9   10
4. Clarity of objectives   1   2   3   4   5   6   7   8   9   10
5. Visual aids   1   2   3   4   5   6   7   8   9   10
6. Handouts   1   2   3   4   5   6   7   8   9   10
7. Value of exercises   1   2   3   4   5   6   7   8   9   10
8. Closing   1   2   3   4   5   6   7   8   9   10

Comments: _____

_____

Delivery

1. Objectives met   1   2   3   4   5   6   7   8   9   10
2. Explanation of main points   1   2   3   4   5   6   7   8   9   10
3. Audience's attention   1   2   3   4   5   6   7   8   9   10
4. Audience involvement   1   2   3   4   5   6   7   8   9   10
5. Voice quality   1   2   3   4   5   6   7   8   9   10
6. Nonverbal communication   1   2   3   4   5   6   7   8   9   10
7. Questions directed to audience   1   2   3   4   5   6   7   8   9   10
8. Answers to audience questions   1   2   3   4   5   6   7   8   9   10
9. Time management   1   2   3   4   5   6   7   8   9   10
10. Feedback   1   2   3   4   5   6   7   8   9   10
11. Speaker's listening skills   1   2   3   4   5   6   7   8   9   10
12. Humor   1   2   3   4   5   6   7   8   9   10

Comments: _____

_____

Facilities

1. Room   1   2   3   4   5   6   7   8   9   10
2. Seating arrangement   1   2   3   4   5   6   7   8   9   10
3. Acoustics   1   2   3   4   5   6   7   8   9   10
4. Lighting   1   2   3   4   5   6   7   8   9   10
5. Equipment   1   2   3   4   5   6   7   8   9   10

Comments: _____

_____

Avoid the temptation to take reviews personally and to defend yourself. Audiences don't care WHY you do something—they only care whether or not it works. Of course, you will run into people who are wrong. The world is full of hostile, angry, or downright crazy people just waiting for the chance to rip into a speaker. But for the most part, most people are just trying to be honest. Remember: you can even learn from a crank if you're willing to listen.

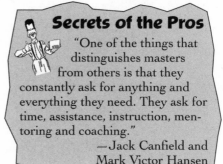

Secrets of the Pros

"One of the things that distinguishes masters from others is that they constantly ask for anything and everything they need. They ask for time, assistance, instruction, mentoring and coaching."

—Jack Canfield and Mark Victor Hansen

What Outsiders Can Do

Seek critics. The best are those who themselves have some training as presenters (or at least frequent listeners). It can come from an association, a coach, a colleague, a friend. Again, when people are criticizing you, ask for detailed critiques. Make sure your critic comments on such things as:

➤ Your delivery

➤ Your appearance and dress

➤ The "feel" of your performance

➤ Any flaws he or she sees

Again, *avoid the temptation to take things personally*. You're out to improve, so it's just business. In any case, you want your critic to be open, honest, not reluctant to give a frank evaluation because you might get mad!

On Work

The key ingredient to improvement is the will to improve, and after that comes work. You don't have to be a workaholic, a millionaire, a Ph.D., a genius, or even all that talented to improve. You just need the will to improve and some character to listen to sometimes unpleasant advice.

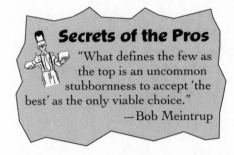

Secrets of the Pros

"What defines the few as the top is an uncommon stubbornness to accept 'the best' as the only viable choice."
— Bob Meintrup

The fact that you've come to the end of this book proves you have the dedication. I believe if you have that, you also have the character to make it happen.

The following pages consist of recommended resources that I hope will be of further value to you.

RECOMMENDED RESOURCES

ASSOCIATIONS

ASTD (AMERICAN SOCIETY FOR TRAINING AND DEVELOPMENT)
Association of trainers—mostly in-house corporate, some contract trainers and consultants. Most cities have monthly lunch or dinner meetings with speakers. Value: information, ideas, industry trends, networking contacts, annual training sessions locally and nationally. 1630 Duke Street, P. O. Box 1443, Alexandria, VA 22313. (703) 683-8100.

NSA (NATIONAL SPEAKERS ASSOCIATION)
Association of professional speakers—individuals, some well-known authors, primarily providing keynote speeches and shorter presentations. Most cities have monthly meetings with speaker. Valuable networking, ideas and information to shorten learning curve. National convention and regional meetings are worth attending. 3877 Seventh Street, Suite 350, Phoenix, AZ 85014. (602) 265-1001.

TOASTMASTERS INTERNATIONAL
The world's largest organization devoted to communication excellence. Through local clubs, Toastmasters offers you the opportunity to learn effective communication through practical experience. In other words, it is a non-profit, self-supporting group of individuals who meet on a regular basis to develop basic speaking skills. Various certifications are available, guided by manuals provided by the national organization. Structure is very valuable, support is excellent. One of the best things you can do to increase your confidence in front of audiences. Very affordable, there is most likely a meeting group in your area. I attended weekly years ago when I entered

this industry—and I recommend it highly. P. O. Box 9052, Mission Viejo, CA 92690. (714) 858-8255.

ISSAC (INTERNATIONAL SOCIETY OF SPEAKERS, AUTHORS, AND CONSULTANTS)
An international organization dedicated to expanding the careers, increasing the effectiveness, and enhancing the lives of speakers, authors, and consultants. P. O. Box 6432, Humble, TX 77525-6432. (800) 6-SPEAKER (677-3253).

SPEAKERS & TRAINERS BUREAUS

WALTERS INTERNATIONAL SPEAKERS BUREAU
Founded by Dottie Walters, a well-known and respected speaking expert. P. O. 1120, Glendora, CA 91740. Contact Lilly Walters at (818) 335-8069 or 1855.

HIGH PERFORMANCE RESOURCES TRAINERS BUREAU
Founded by Tony Jeary, providing train-the-trainer services, career consultations and specialized training. HPR works primarily with large communication agencies matching the right people (speakers, trainers and consultants) to the right projects. 3001 LBJ Freeway, Suite 240, Dallas, TX 75234. Call Reg Cavender at (800) 982-2509.

MAGAZINES

Sharing Ideas, a top independent publication in the field of professional speaking. P. O. 1120, Glendora, CA 91740. (818) 335-8069 or 1855.

Training, a monthly publication focusing on the latest news, ideas, and technology for training adults. Lakewood Publications, 50 S. Ninth Street, Minneapolis, MN 55402.

Presentations, a monthly publication, focuses mostly on technology available for making presentations. Lakewood Publications, 50 S. Ninth Street, Minneapolis, MN 55402.

NEWSLETTERS

Inspire Any Audience Newsletter, produced by High Performance Resources, offers the reader updated information and tips on making powerful presentations. 3001 LBJ Freeway, Suite 240, Dallas, TX 75234. Call (214) 484-9627.

CATALOGS

Pfeiffer & Company International Publishers—They offer books, videos, and seminar kits for the human resources professional and trainers. Call (800) 274-4434.

Training Ideas: Resource Guide & Product Catalog (Talico Incorporated)—Offers a wide range of resources such as climate surveys, supervisory skill tests, training videos and books, training games and exercises, and more. Call (904) 241-1721.

HRD Press—Aimed directly at the human resource development market, HRD Press offers workshop kits, games, computer-based training, books, videos, and more. Call (800) 822-2801.

Recommended Resources (Lakewood Publications)—One of the most comprehensive collections of tools for training and presenting. Call (800) 707-7769.

CRM Films, Video Training Resources. They offer a variety of video rental tapes on such subjects as decision making, customer service, empowerment, leadership and more. High content, entertaining storylines, and each tape is accompanied by comprehensive instructional materials. They even offer free previews. Call for a free catalog: (800) 421-0833.

BOOKS

Flip Charts: How to Draw Them and How to Use Them, Richard Brandt (Pfeiffer & Company, ISBN 0-88390-031-9). A handbook of practical things that work when using flip charts. Easy to read and easy to use. Call (619) 578-5900 or fax (619) 578-2042.

Creative Training Techniques, Robert Pike (Lakewood Publications, ISBN 0-94321-06-2). Bob Pike is well known in the training industry as a leader when it comes to presentation creative input. He also holds fantastic seminars and publishes a great newsletter. Call Lakewood Publications at (612) 333-0471.

You've Got to be Believed to be Heard, Bert Decker (St. Martins Press, ISBN 0-312-09949-5). This very unique book is a must for the serious presenter who wants to increase audience buy-in and believability. Decker Communications offers a newsletter, tapes, and seminars. Call (800) 547-0050 or (415) 391-5544.

Money Talks: The Complete Guide to Creating a Profitable Workshop or Seminar in Any Field, and *How to Make a Whole Lot More Than $1,000,000 Writing . . .,* Dr. Jeffrey Lant (Jeffrey Lant Associates, ISBN 0-940374-26-9). These books is packed with creative ideas to make money and improve your skills. Dr. Lant has a variety of other very useful books and special reports. Call him—95% of the time, he answers his own phone—(617) 547-6372; fax (617) 738-0885. (See the special offer in the back of this book for additional items Jeffrey has agreed to offer my readers.)

How to Get Your Point Across in 30 Seconds—or Less, Milo O. Frank (Simon & Schuster, ISBN 0-671-52492-5). The common ability of most efficient managers and leaders in every business and profession is the ability to present themselves and their ideas effectively. This book shows us how to make the most of every opportunity.

Secrets of Successful Speakers, Lilly Walters (McGraw-Hill, ISBN 0-07-068033-7). The title says it all. This book is full of ideas to help you take your next speech or presentation to the next level.

The Secrets of Charisma, Doe Lang (SPI Books, ISBN 0-944007-41-4). What is that intangible "something" that sets great leaders and presenters apart? Charisma! This book tells how to develop and use it. An audio is also available.

The Leader's Edge, Sandy Linver (Simon & Schuster, ISBN 0-684-80433-6). This book is not a "how-to" book—it is a "where to" book, about where communicate development can. You can contact Linver's company, Speakeasy, Inc. at (404) 261-4029.

The Greatest Speakers I Ever Heard, Dottie Walters (WRS, ISBN 1-56796-052-9). Dottie is one of the co-founders of the National Speakers Association and an incredible resource; be sure to get all of her books, tapes, and programs. Walters International Speakers Bureau, 18825 Hicreast Road, Glendale, CA 91741. (818) 335-8069. (For other information Dottie has agreed to provide my readers, see the special offer in the back of this book.)

How to Make It Big in the Seminar Business, Paul Kavasik (McGraw-Hill, ISBN 0-07-033185-5). Paul has specialized in the seminar business, founding ASLA, the American Seminar Leaders Association. The seminar business is one of the most lucrative, glamorous, and prestigious entrepreneurial opportunities available in America today.

How to Have the Awesome Power of Public Speaking, Peter Daniels (House of Tabor, ISBN 0-949330-25-6). Peter Daniels outlines different areas of public speaking from the perspective of the speaker's power and responsibility with an audience.

How to Present Like a Pro, Lani Arredondo (McGraw-Hill, ISBN 0-07-002506-1). This is a practical guide for making persuasive presentations. It's basic premise: "Information alone doesn't persuade people; strong presentation skills do."

I Can See You Naked, Ron Hoff (Andrews & McMeel, ISBN 0-8362-8000-8).

Presentations Plus, David Peoples (John Wiley & Sons, ISBN 0-471-55956-3). Regardless of your audience, this book offers many useful strategies, guidelines, and principles you can use to present, persuade, and win.

you^2, Price Pritchett, Ph.D. (Quicksilver Press, ISBN 0-944002-04). Making a quantum leap—going from you to you^2—means accomplishing far more, in far less time, with only a fraction of the effort you've been giving. Price Pritchett introduces us to the power of taking quantum leaps in this booklet available from Pritchett & Associates, Inc. by calling (800) 992-5922.

The Quantum Leap Strategy, Price Pritchett, Ph.D. (Quicksilver Press, ISBN 0-944002-08-0). Price Pritchett has very effectively focused on a variety of small booklets which have positioned him in the marketplace as an expert. This booklet is the sequel to *you^2* and further explains the unconventional set of behaviors that will bring you breakthrough performance by showing you how to make quantum leaps in productivity, quality and overall performance. This booklet is also available from Pritchett & Associates, Inc. by calling (800) 992-5922.

5 Secrets to Personal Productivity, Hanks and Pulsipher (Franklin, ISBN 0-939817-05-5). You can find this little book at one of my favorite resources, Franklin Quest, the creator of the Franklin Day Planner. This book is to the point and very valuable if increasing your results is important to you. For a catalog, time-management seminars, or the store nearest you, call (800) 654-1776.

How to Argue and Win Every Time, Gerry Spence (St. Martins Press, ISBN 0-312-11827-9). Gerry Spence is a courtroom attorney who has never lost a case. His premise is that presentation success is based on credibility.

Raving Fans, Blanchard and Bowles (Morris, ISBN 0-688-12316-3). Ken Blanchard, known for his phenomenal best seller *The One Minute Manager,* has done it again with *Raving Fans.* If you have not read it, you need to. Your raving fans are the key to your future business and success.

Training Managers to Train, Bro. Herman E. Zuccarolli, CSC (Crisp, ISBN 0-931961-43-2). Part of the Crisp Fifty-Minute™ Series, this book focuses on answering the question: How exactly does a manager prepare for, plan, present, and follow up on training programs designed to yield competent employees? Crisp has books and videos available in the Fifty-Minute™ Series. Call (800) 442-7477 for a free catalog.

Facilitation Skills for Team Leaders, Donald Hackett, Ph.D. and Charles L. Martin, Ph.D. (Crisp, ISBN 1-56052-199-6). Another in Crisp's Fifty-Minute™ Series, this book is a resource that will help people who are placed in the roles of facilitators build their skills to become more effective team leaders. Call Crisp at (800) 442-7477 for this book and a copy of their catalog.

The Spellbinder's Gift, Og Mandino (Fawcett Columbine, ISBN 0-449-90690-6). Og Mandino is a treasure among authors, a writer who infuses human relationships with the energy of the divine, the light of the miraculous. In this book, he tells the story of a retired motivational speakers' agent and God's calling him back into the work he had done all of his life.

Speak and Grow Rich, Dottie Walters and Lilly Walters (Prentice Hall, ISBN 0-13-825803-1). In this book, Dottie and Lilly have included all the techniques and shortcuts that today's top speakers use to generate fees of up to $800,000 and more! Earl Nightingale calls this book ". . . a first-class book for budding speakers. It is also a first-class book for professional speakers . . ."

What to Say When . . . You're Dying on the Platform, Lilly Walters (McGraw-Hill, ISBN 0-07-068039-6). Turn to this "First-Aid Kit" for the quips, "saver" lines, and practical preventive strategies that will rescue your speech from hecklers, equipment breakdown, late arrivals (including yours), loud noises, missing props, and more!

Powerful Presentation Skills, Debra Smith (CareerTrack Publications). This is a step-by-step workbook that walks you through the process of building a powerful presentation. Call CareerTrack Publications about this workbook, seminars, or a free catalog at (800) 334-6780.

Even More Games Trainers Play, Edward E. Scannell and John W. Newstrom (McGraw-Hill, ISBN 0-07-046414-6). This is the forth in a series of "Games Trainers Play" books. They are all full of hundreds of activities, brain-teasers, and games that will positively increase the effectiveness of your next presentation.

How to Speak Like a Pro, Leon Fletcher (Ballantine, ISBN 0-345-33427-2). This book offers step-by-step strategies for developing the confidence to speak well anywhere—from the board room to the PTA meeting.

Secrets of Successful Speakers, Lilly Walters (McGraw-Hill, ISBN 0-07-068033-7). Lilly Walters outlines 11 easy steps to mastering the secrets of the most successful speakers of our day.

Speaker's Sourcebook II, Glenn Van Ekeren (Prentice Hall, ISBN 0-13-825225-4). This is a unique collection of fresh and relevant stories and anecdotes that will delight any audience. Call People Building Institute at (712) 324-4873.

Speaking Magic, Carolyn Dickson (Oakhill Press, ISBN 0-9619590-8-8). This is a fast-reading book on the keys to taking control in front of the room. Call VOICE-PRO (216) 932-8040.

What to Say and How to Say It, David Belson (Citadel Press, ISBN 0-8065-1447-7). This handbook provides examples of things to say for the most frequent situations you face, such as weddings, retirements, dedications, birthdays, etc.

Endless Referrals, Bob Burg (McGraw-Hill, ISBN 0-07-008942-6). This is a great book on how to network your everyday contacts into sales and set yourself apart in today's sell-saturated world of junk faxes and telemarketing.

See You at the Top, Zig Ziglar (Pelican Publishing, ISBN 0-88289-126-X). To order, call (214) 233-9191, ext. 109. This is Zig's cornerstone book, just one of the twelve outstanding books he has written and one of the most influential books I've ever read.

AUDIO TAPES (ALBUMS)

Speak to Win, Bert Decker (Nightingale-Conant Corporation). Bert Decker covers the 12 areas of speaking in this six-cassette audio program. For more information or to order, call Nightingale-Conant at (800) 323-5552.

The Compleat Speaker, Earl Nightingale (Nightingale-Conant Corporation). This advanced, comprehensive six-cassette program covers every facet — in just about every possible situation — of public speaking. To order, call Nightingale-Conant at (800) 323-5552.

The 7 Fee Ranges of the Speaking & Training Industry, Juanell Teague (PeoplePlus). A powerful evaluation and planning tool to help determine what fees to charge to match your worth and protect your credibility. For more details, see the special offer in the back of this book. To order, call (214) 484-9627.

WORKSHOP

Inspire Any Audience Workshop. An in-house customized workshop for six to fifty people. Contact High Performance Resources at (800) 982-2509.

PRODUCTS

Pierce Business Products provides an effective tool to help you make presentations in quality style. The Presenter flipchart easel helps you look professional by giving you the versatility and flexibility that you need to address any group effectively. This tool is featured on the back cover of the book. I have used one for years and highly recommend this tool to you. Call Pierce Business Products at (800) 372-7377 or write them at Three Bryan Drive, Wheeling, WV 26003.

The TUMI 243D 22-inch wheel-a-way is what I use as my trainer's toolbox. This is the best rolling bag I've owned. Contact TUMI Luggage, 250 Lackland Dr., Middlesex, NJ 08846. (908) 271-9500.

The laser pointer that I am holding in my hand on the front cover is by Lyte Optronics. This has become an invaluable part of my toolbox. Call Lyte Optronics at (310) 450-8551.

Mr. Sketch scented markers are the only choice for working with flip charts. The smell of traditional markers can literally make people ill.

199

I buy these markers by the dozen to make me and my audience more comfortable during presentations. Call Sanford at 800-438-3703.

Post-it™ Easel Pads and Easel Rolls help enhance communications in meetings and presentations. These pads, which are simply flipchart-sized Post-it™ notes, allow you to focus on the content of your meetings and are great for posting completed flipchart pages around the room without damaging walls or other surfaces. 3M Commercial Office Supply Division, P. O. Box 130514, Roseville, MN 55113-9759.

PEOPLE

Presentation Coaches can be reached by contacting Reg Cavender at 800-982-2509.

John Bacon, Ann Arbor, Michigan

Sherry Boecher, Overland Park, Kansas

Judy Chaffee, Naperville, Illinois

Richard Clipp, Overland Park, Kansas

Fred Collins, Colleyville, Texas

Rick Davis, McKinney, Texas

Dave Freeborn, Simpsonville, South Carolina

Derek Green, Ann Arbor, Michigan

Myra Ketterman, Mountain Rest, South Carolina

Doug Kevorkian, Ann Arbor, Michigan

Lindsay Lowe, Marietta, Georgia

Bob Meintrup, Edwardsville, Illinois

Patrick O'Dooley, Dallas, Texas

Mark Pantak, Dallas, Texas

Steve Richards, Chamblee, Georgia

Tim Salladay, Bedford, Texas

Tony Walker, Overland Park, Kansas

Dale Ware, Houston, Texas

PROMOTIONS

The following pages contain promotions which I believe will be of special interest to you.

Speakers & Trainers — If you price yourself too low, you hurt your credibility; if your fees outrun your real value you risk more permanent damage.

Plug *your* personal information into this powerful evaluation and planning tool. For just $29.95, you can *take control of your career!* **To order call (214) 484-9627.**

7 Fee Ranges of the $peaking & Training Industry

The 7 Fee Ranges of the Speaking & Training Industry will show you:

- How to determine what you're worth now.

- What to do next to be worth more.

- How to organize your leaps from part-time to full-time to **big-time!**

- Each level's pitfalls and hidden leverages.

"In less than an hour you can determine what your speaking fee should be now . . . and 10 years from now!"
— Juanell Teague

A special offer from
Dr. Jeffrey Lant

Resource #1: FREE subscription to Jeffrey Lant's twice-monthly WORLDGRAM Newsletter.

In addition to his books and quarterly publications and card decks, Dr. Lant is making available to you a FREE subscription to his WORLDGRAM Newsletter. It is packed with business-building information of all kinds, with a particular emphasis on today's successful marketing bambits, including the World Wide Web. To activate your free subscription, email your email address to incor@oanet.com. Your subscription will start within 10 days!

Resource #2: Promote your book, booklet, audio cassette, video cassette, etc. in Jeffrey's WORLDGRAM Newsletter and WORLDPROFIT ONLINE CATALOG.

Dr. Jeffrey Lant, a leader in card-deck and Internet marketing, has now developed a new source of product sales through his WORLD-GRAM Newsletter and WORLDPROFIT ONLINE CATALOG.

If you have products to sell, do the following:

- Send Jeffrey a copy of your media release. Assuming the product is of general interest to businesses or consumers, he wants to sell it in his online newsletter/catalog.

- In this case, you take your media release and order form and email it to him at incor@oanet.com or send it on IBM-compatible diskette. Give him the retail price of your product and the amount you want for both U.S. and foreign shipping. Send the IBM-compatible diskette to:

    > Worldprofit, Inc.
    > ATTN: George Kosch
    > 9010-106 Avenue, Suite 208
    > Edmonton, Alta T5H 4K3
    > Canada

- Jeffrey will email this information around the world and collect all orders, taking a 50% discount. 50% of the retail purchase price plus applicable shipping and customer name will be sent to you. You ship the product direct.

- This offer is available to you for as many products as you have.

This chapter reveals:

➤ The Top Secrets from the book on tear-out cards for further study.

Glossary of Terms

Anecdote

A short story used during a presentation to illustrate or emphasize a point.

Articulation

Clear, concise formation of consonant and vowel sounds. Articulation results in speech that is easy for the audience to understand.

Audience

People that a presenter addresses. Can be one or more people. (See *Participants*.)

Body

The middle portion of a presentation. This section develops and supports the main concepts of thorough use of information, activities, and other material.

Body Language

Mannerisms or gestures used for the purpose of emphasizing a point. Studies show that success in a presentation depends about 7% on the words spoken, 38% on the tone of the words spoken and 55% on the body language of the speaker.

Business Entertainment

The use of activities, games, or role playing during a presentation to counter a short attention span. Usually, these activities are placed at five- to six-minute intervals.

Cliché

Standard phrases or comparisons that have become trite from overuse.

Communication

The social process of defining concepts and information through use of symbols. Can be written, verbal, or nonverbal.

Conclusion

Final section of a presentation during which main concepts are summarized and reemphasized.

Connotation
Attitude or emotion associated with a word; an overtone. (See *Denotation.*)

Continuous Improvement
Commitment to using audience feedback and other forms of criticism to continually improve presentation skills.

Credibility
A speaker's believability. A credible speaker is one that has the trust and confidence of the audience.

Culture
Traditions and lifestyles of a group of people.

Deductive Reasoning
A process of reasoning that bases conclusions on a general rule. Individual examples are explained and justified by the rule. (See *Inductive Reasoning.*)

Denotation
Literal dictionary meaning of a word; a word's definition.

Diaphragm
Muscle separating the chest from the abdomen. Control over this muscle result in improved breathing and speaking ability.

Empathic Listening
Listening that occurs when an audience identifies with a speaker and gives emotional support.

Evaluative Listening
A type of listening that results in a decision-making process.

Evidence
Facts, statistics, or any other form of data that supports a thesis.

Eye Contact
Making direct visual contact with members of the audience. Eye contact develops trust and credibility.

Facilitator

One who simplifies information so that the audience can easily understand concepts and relationships. Incorporates games, role playing, and other interactive methods to involve the audience.

Feedback

Response of audience to presentation.

Four Audience Tensions

In every presentation, four sources of tension exist: audience to presenter, audience to environment, audience to audience, and audience to material.

Funneling

Processing of all possible presentation material to arrive at three major objectives that will be presented.

Identification

Ability of an audience to relate to presentation; perception that speaker is similar to them and is trustworthy.

Impromptu Speaking

Speaking with little or no preparation and no use of notes.

Inductive Reasoning

Process of reasoning that uses specific examples to explain a general rule.

Infer

Use a generalization to imply a meaning.

Informative Presentation

Seeks to expand audience knowledge by defining concepts and relationships.

Inspire

Unique ability of a speaker to move an audience. Listeners not only hear words, but act upon them.

Instructor

Speaker or presenter that provides information or instruction to an audience. May or may not use visual aids. May or may not use interactive methods.

Introduction
Beginning of a presentation. Section that states purpose and provides preview of material that will be covered.

Lecturer
Speaker or presenter that provides information to audience. Communication is, generally, one way.

Participants
In an interactive presentation, the audience members are referred to as participants. The term reflects the dynamic and interactive atmosphere that a presentation seeks to create.

Perception
Meaning given to the understanding of concepts. Generally, does not incorporate interactive method.

Persuasive Presentation
Presentation that seeks to move audience to particular action or belief.

Prejudice
Preconceived notion, opinion, or judgment regarding a person or group.

Presentation
Speaking to one or more people to present concepts and relationships in an interactive and dynamic manner.

Presenter
Presents material to audience, generally with use of visual aids and activities that involve the audience.

Public Communication
Communication with a large group. One person speaks as an audience listens.

Speaker
Delivers information while audience listens. Generally, audience participation is minimal.

Speech
Lecture-oriented means of delivering information.

Speech Communication

Sending and receiving oral messages for the purpose of creating meaning.

Subconscious Desires

Needs or wants that nearly all of us share. They include: to belong, to be respected, to be liked, to be safe, to succeed, to find romance, to be inspired.

Targeted Polling

Means of monitoring individual audience responses. Seeking feedback from particular individuals.

Testimonial

Endorsement of person, place, or thing. Usually, celebrities are used.

Trainer

Trains audience to perform a skill. Usually, through hands-on practice.

Verbal Survey

Method of monitoring audience response during a presentation.

Visual Aid

Any audio or visual aid to a presentation. Charts, maps, graphs, tapes, movies, overhead projections, slides, and flip charts are common visual aids.

Index

211

Index

A Message from Tony Jeary

It's been said that persuasion is the art of creating psychological momentum. If that's correct, then perfecting this art is something for which The Zig Ziglar Corporation has long been known through its comprehensive two-day *Effective Business Presentations* seminar.

Literally thousands of people have learned to speak with greater confidence, competence, and comfort by mastering the twelve powerful presentation skills taught in *Effective Business Presentations*. Here are a few highlights Mr. Ziglar has provided from the program; I believe this blends perfectly with *Inspire Any Audience*.

❑ Increase power to influence other people in management, sales, human resources
❑ Develop flexibility in communication patterns with people nationally and internationally
❑ Learn correct speaker's stance
❑ Learn to demonstrate confidence by using extended eye contact
❑ Learn how to utilize vocal variety and get rid of whiny, nasal sound
❑ Rid speech of padding that sometimes adds sound, but no meaning
❑ Learn what constitutes good audience interaction
❑ Practice Question & Answer sessions; they can make or break presentations
❑ Implement effective use of humor
❑ Learn how and when visual aids add value

And in Zig Ziglar terms, keep working on your sales and
presentation skills and he will see you
"OVER THE TOP!"

APPENDIX
Reproducible Pages

AUDIENCE WORKSHEET

What sort of knowledge about my topic do they bring to the table?

_____

_____

_____

Will they be for me or against me? Why?

_____

_____

_____

List of people whom they admire in their organization and are most likely to admire outside of it:

_____

_____

_____

Things that have worked with similar audiences in the past—and things that haven't:

_____

_____

_____

Why was I asked to present?

_____

_____

_____

This page may be reproduced without permission.

THE PRESENTATION WORK ORDER

Title of Presentation _____

Date of Presentation _____

How much time do I have to prepare? _____

How much time will I have to speak? _____

What kind of room will I be speaking in?

❑ Conference room   ❑ Living room

❑ Boardroom   ❑ Other _____

❑ Classroom

How many people will I be speaking to? _____

What type of financial budget is available?

❑ Large budget—lots of money, as in   <u>$ Let's do it right!</u>
"Money is no (big) object."

❑ Small budget—money is available $_____
but is definitely an object.

❑ No budget—money isn't an object $____0____
because there's none to spend.

What type of equipment will be available to me?

❑ Flip chart(s)?   ❑ Overhead projector?

❑ Tape player?   ❑ VCR and monitor?

❑ Advanced presentation   ❑ Chairs and tables?
hardware and software?

❑ Other _____

What type of equipment do I need to provide / rent? _____

_____

What about handouts? _____

_____

This page may be reproduced without permission.

THREE-DIMENSIONAL OUTLINE

Title of Presentation: _____

Objectives:

- _____
- _____
- _____

Time	Who	Segment	What	Why	How

CHECKLIST FOR EFFECTIVE REHEARSAL

Well before your presentation:

Prepare and mentally walk-through:

❏ 3-D outline

❏ Each section of presentation

❏ 3x5 cards

Rehearse in front of :

❏ Other people

❏ Video camera

❏ Mirror

Just before your presentation:

Locate and know how to operate
the following fixtures:

❏ Electrical outlets

❏ Lighting controls

❏ Volume controls for room sound

❏ Window-blind cords

Locate the following:

❏ Restrooms

❏ Telephones

❏ Stairs and elevators

❏ Smoking areas

Comments:

_____

_____

_____

_____

_____

_____

_____

_____

PRESENTATION ASSESSMENT

Skill/Traits	1	2	3	4	5	6	7	8	9	10

Preparation:

Analyzing audience — — — — — — — — — —

Developing objectives — — — — — — — — — —

Developing visual aids — — — — — — — — — —

Checking logistics — — — — — — — — — —

Overcoming nervousness — — — — — — — — — —

Stating main ideas — — — — — — — — — —

Deciding supporting information — — — — — — — — — —

Creating an opener — — — — — — — — — —

Developing transitions — — — — — — — — — —

Structuring the main body — — — — — — — — — —

Using visual aids — — — — — — — — — —

Preparing the close — — — — — — — — — —

Delivery:

Vocal image

Volume — — — — — — — — — —

Pace — — — — — — — — — —

Pausing — — — — — — — — — —

Verbal image

Vocabulary — — — — — — — — — —

Grammar — — — — — — — — — —

Pronunciation — — — — — — — — — —

Visual image

Dress/Appearance — — — — — — — — — —

Posture — — — — — — — — — —

Gestures — — — — — — — — — —

Eye contact — — — — — — — — — —

Facial expressions/Smile — — — — — — — — — —

Challenging situations:

Handling questions — — — — — — — — — —

Managing mishaps — — — — — — — — — —

Controlling problem people — — — — — — — — — —

BODY LANGUAGE EVALUATION

Title _____ Name of Evaluator _____ Date _____

NOTE TO THE EVALUATOR: In this presentation the speaker is concentrating on body language. He or she should use gestures, facial expressions, and other body movements that illustrate and enhance the verbal message. In evaluating this speech, focus on delivery rather than content. Use a rating scale of 1 to 10, where 1 represents unsatisfactory and 10 indicates outstanding.

Action	Rating	Comments
Preparation	1 2 3 4 5 6 7 8 9 10	_____
Organization	1 2 3 4 5 6 7 8 9 10	_____
Appearance	1 2 3 4 5 6 7 8 9 10	_____
Topic	1 2 3 4 5 6 7 8 9 10	_____
Manner	1 2 3 4 5 6 7 8 9 10	_____
Body movements	1 2 3 4 5 6 7 8 9 10	_____
Posture	1 2 3 4 5 6 7 8 9 10	_____
Gestures	1 2 3 4 5 6 7 8 9 10	_____
Eye contact	1 2 3 4 5 6 7 8 9 10	_____
Facial expressions	1 2 3 4 5 6 7 8 9 10	_____

POST-PRESENTATION EVALUATION

Instructions: Read each group and circle the number that most closely describes how effective the presentation was in each respective area. Use a rating scale of 1 to 10 in which 1 represents unsatisfactory and 10 indicates outstanding.

Preparation and Content

1. Opening	1	2	3	4	5	6	7	8	9	10
2. Content material	1	2	3	4	5	6	7	8	9	10
3. Organization of material	1	2	3	4	5	6	7	8	9	10
4. Clarity of objectives	1	2	3	4	5	6	7	8	9	10
5. Visual aids	1	2	3	4	5	6	7	8	9	10
6. Handouts	1	2	3	4	5	6	7	8	9	10
7. Value of exercises	1	2	3	4	5	6	7	8	9	10
8. Closing	1	2	3	4	5	6	7	8	9	10

Comments: _____

_____

Delivery

1. Objectives met	1	2	3	4	5	6	7	8	9	10
2. Explanation of main points	1	2	3	4	5	6	7	8	9	10
3. Audience's attention	1	2	3	4	5	6	7	8	9	10
4. Audience involvement	1	2	3	4	5	6	7	8	9	10
5. Voice quality	1	2	3	4	5	6	7	8	9	10
6. Nonverbal communication	1	2	3	4	5	6	7	8	9	10
7. Questions directed to audience	1	2	3	4	5	6	7	8	9	10
8. Answers to audience questions	1	2	3	4	5	6	7	8	9	10
9 Time management	1	2	3	4	5	6	7	8	9	10
10. Feedback	1	2	3	4	5	6	7	8	9	10
11. Speaker's listening skills	1	2	3	4	5	6	7	8	9	10
12. Humor	1	2	3	4	5	6	7	8	9	10

Comments: _____

_____

Facilities

1. Room	1	2	3	4	5	6	7	8	9	10
2. Seating arrangement	1	2	3	4	5	6	7	8	9	10
3. Acoustics	1	2	3	4	5	6	7	8	9	10
4. Lighting	1	2	3	4	5	6	7	8	9	10
5. Equipment	1	2	3	4	5	6	7	8	9	10

Comments: _____

_____

This page may be reproduced without permission.